CREATIVE QUILTING
FOR
HOME DECOR

ALSO BY LINDA DENNER

with photography by Leonard Denner

BABY QUILTS:

30 Full-Color Patterns in Patchwork and Appliqué,
Worked by Hand and Machine Quilting

CREATIVE
QUILTING
FOR
HOME DECOR

LINDA DENNER

Photographs by Leonard Denner

CROWN TRADE PAPERBACKS   NEW YORK

Published by Crown Trade Paperbacks, Inc., 201 East 50th Street, New York,
New York 10022. Member of the Crown Publishing Group.

Random House, Inc. New York, Toronto, London, Sydney, Auckland

CROWN TRADE PAPERBACKS and colophon are trademarks of
Crown Publishers, Inc.

Manufactured in Hong Kong

Design by June Bennett-Tantillo

Library of Congress Cataloging-in-Publication Data

Denner, Linda.

Creative quilting for home decor / by Linda Denner ; photographs

by Leonard Denner. — 1st ed.

p. cm.

1. Machine quilting—Patterns.
2. Quilted goods. 3. Drapery.
4. Household linens. I. Title.

TT835.D454 1995   94-8647

746.46—dc20   CIP

ISBN 0-517-88142-X

10 9 8 7 6 5 4 3 2 1

First Edition

HOME

Grace Groening

I long not for wealth or great success,

*A cozy fireside, friends are all I wish to
possess:*

I don't yearn for a mansion great,

*Where one's humble friends are made to
wait.*

Just a cheery spot at the close of day,

Where I may relax, my troubles allay;

A welcome on the door to my friends who may roam,

*To my little paradise, the place I call
Home.*

CONTENTS

PART 4: SHADES 87

GLOSSARY OF PROCEDURES 99

ACKNOWLEDGMENTS

I wish to thank the following organizations for their assistance:

Pfaff American Sales, Paramus, New Jersey

Freudenberg, Pellon Division, New York, New York

Pryn/Dritz, Spartanburg, South Carolina

The Crowning Touch Inc., Medford, Oregon

Concord Fabrics, New York, New York

Elna Inc., Eden Prairie, Minnesota

INTRODUCTION

I began my first quilt in 1974, and I have enjoyed every aspect of this craft since that first modest project. I have made pieced, appliquéd, Log Cabin, string-pieced, mixed-medium, hand-quilted, and machine-quilted bedcoverings nonstop over this twenty-year period. Before my interest in quilting, I sewed clothing for myself, my mother, and my two daughters. I was most content with a needle in my hand, and have now spent forty-plus years in the pursuit of happiness. In the past decade I have resorted to making all the curtains and drapery items for our home. In the space of two hours I could have precisely the size, color, and style window treatment that I desired without falling victim to the poorly constructed, overpriced, and limited selection available in ready-made. If you have never made a curtain before, you will be delighted at the speed and simplicity of the process. You can seam, pleat, or smock, with the precision of a skilled professional, new products that require no sewing. This is indeed an ideal way to stretch and build your sewing machine skills as you transform your home into a showcase.

Combining simple construction techniques with quilting basics, we have entered a new study of needle arts I will call "Decorative Quilting." I assume that you have made or purchased a quilt for your bed and are seeking a uniformity of design in the room. To this end I will offer multiple solutions, all created within a few short hours. The valance designs provided in this text are wonderful in combination with curtains you may already have on hand, either purchased or sewn yourself. With the freedom allowed by new products made specifically for home decor, I have included pieced and appliquéd window shades. What could offer more delight to a child than a night shade featuring a dreamland scene?

Many techniques shown in these pages are new, such as the removable and interchangeable lampshades. Within an hour you can cover and revitalize an old lamp to match and accent a room. Since these shades take so little time and effort, I hope that my instructions and designs start you off on a fanciful flurry of activity creating shades for holidays and special occasions. Room did not permit its inclusion in this text, but I know I intend to make a Halloween lampshade with a pumpkin to glow in the window.

Finally, since my skills and interests are closely associated with my sewing machine and serger, appropriate instructions for their use in home decor projects are given in the Glossary. When you are creating home decorating projects, speed, ease, and durability are essential. The modern sewing machine and serger are the ideal tools for this job.

Feel free to use some of the treasured quilting fabric that you have on hand, but do not limit yourself to the 100% cotton palette reserved for your quilts. Decorator fabrics are more fade-resistant and color-fast. Their additional width of 54″ can be an aid to construction. When you use standard calico fabric, it is important to line your work. You can use muslin, solid sheets, or decorator lining fabric. A window that appears to get a small amount of sunlight will begin to fade your cottons in less than twenty-five hours of daylight. All the valances contained in this text have batting as well as muslin linings.

I am certain you will find satisfaction in adding quilting touches to every room of your house. I hope that you will enjoy as much pleasure in stitching the projects for your home as I have had in designing and writing this book.

PART ONE

QUILTED CURTAINS

Every quilter has an assortment of prints on hand that can be incorporated into this charming window treatment. This is the ideal project to use up the odds and ends remaining from other projects that are a bit too much to simply put out for the trash. Select a good variety of light, medium, and dark values. You can limit your palette to one color family or use every color available, yielding a window treatment with a truly country flair. Before you start your project decide the method of construction you wish to follow. With the use of a serger or overlock machine equipped with a roll hem attachment you can serge your fabric together while decoratively finishing the raw edges in one operation. Check the Glossary for more specific directions for Piecing on a Serger. With a conventional machine, cut the fabric with a rotary cutter and stitch, using an assembly-line method. For conventional seaming you will be lining the entire curtain to prevent wear from laundering on the standard $1/4''$ seams. This lining will also prevent fading. The Glossary provides a sequence, Lining a Curtain and Preparing the Header; refer to this section for detailed information.

1

COUNTRY PATCHWORK CURTAINS

MATERIALS

Assorted prints and solid cotton or polycotton cut into 3″ × 5″ rectangular shapes. This shape's measurement may vary with the available pieces used and according to your own visual judgment. By maintaining a rectangular shape, the curtain will present a pleasing conformity of shape to the window. Match sewing or serger thread to the fabric. The total yardage of the curtain project must be accommodated by the patches on hand. For example, if you need 3 yards of fabric for the lower curtain of your window treatment, you may need 12 quarter-yard lengths, 24 eighth-yard cuts, or whatever amount yields the yardage when sewn together.

Shirring tape for the curtain header. Use Dritz™ Iron-on Pleater Tape, Montserrat™ tape or Gosling™ tape to ensure an even gathering of pleats along the top edge. Purchase a sufficient length of shirring tape to be attached to the entire top edge of curtain width.

INSTRUCTIONS

1. Measure the window size. For standard 44″-width fabric, use one width of 44″ or 54″ for each curtain panel cut to the window length. Add a ¼″ seam allowance to all your measurements. Since your yardage will be made up of patches to accommodate the width and length required for each panel, seam the rectangles together until they are of sufficient size for each curtain panel. For example, if the window is 36″ × 54″, add 3¼″ to the header that will include the casing, hems, and shirring tape. Measure the length of the window and add the 3¼″ to this number. If you plan

on trimming the curtain with a ruffle, include its size into the finished curtain length. For example, with a 54″ window opening, I choose a finished length of 63″. Add $3\frac{1}{4}$″ to 63″ for $66\frac{1}{4}$″ in length. When attaching a 4″ ruffle to the lower edge, cut $3\frac{3}{4}$″ less than the $66\frac{1}{4}$″ length. The additional $\frac{1}{2}$″ is for the $\frac{1}{4}$″ attaching seam allowance. Curtains should be $2\frac{1}{2}$ times the window width. This is extremely full and may be decreased to twice the width when using medium- to heavy-weight fabric. Utilizing the fabric width of 44″ or 54″ for one panel of your curtain pairs will be convenient. When constructing curtains for windows of double or triple width, seam the sections together. Be careful to match patterns, and sew the sections together to allow for a convenient rod opening. Since you are customizing the curtain construction, make as many openings as you need.

2. The curtain illustrated was constructed by a serger using a three-thread rolled hem. I found it most convenient to precut all the fabric to a 3″ × 5″ rectangle. With the application of an overlocked rolled hem, I quickly attached all the vertical rows of prints together and completed the assembly by serging the rows together. Use a Woolly Nylon™ thread in the upper looper in a matching color for the best seam coverage. Maintain the seams right sides out to display the rolled hem, or position them with wrong side together to conceal the rolled hem. Refer to Piecing on a Serger in the Glossary.

3. Prepare a ruffle for the curtain. Refer to New Options for Gathering Ruffles in the Glossary for hints on ruffle construction.

4. In selecting the fabric, remember that your color values should be harmonious. Since your window treatment will be viewed from a distance of at least five feet, do not concern yourself with coordinating small prints. They will be unnoticeable to the viewer. Use a wide selection of print scale and texture to provide variety for the eye.

5. Serge the pieces together by aligning the wrong sides of the fabric facing each other. Use decorative thread in the loopers for accent.

6. The sides and top of the curtain are finished with a rolled hem. Sew the ruffle to the lower edge with a rolled hem or an overlock stitch. For the conventional sewing machine, attach the ruffle with an overcasting stitch. If your machine has only a straight stitch, bind the seam. This will protect the seam from wear through frequent laundering.

7. Sew a casing following the suggestions in Installing Pleater or Shirring Tape in the Glossary to complete the curtain.

2
VERTICAL STRIPPED CURTAINS

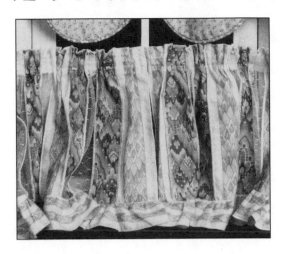

This treatment is wonderful when incorporating stripped fabric in a patchwork curtain. Select coordinating prints and consider the lovely effect of a lace insert. A light Victorian feeling is created with this window treatment. This is another important opportunity to utilize a serger or overlock machine. For conventional sewing machines, a French seam would provide durability in construction. Lining the curtain is an option, but the pleasing effect of the lace insert will be lost with a lining. Refer to the Glossary for French Seams.

MATERIALS

The yardage requirement for this project will be determined by the curtain length you require as well as by the width of the window. If the curtain will be 36" in length without the attachment of a ruffle, you will need 39¼" to accommodate the header, length, and seam allowances. If your window requires two panels of 44"-wide cloth, and you are using a combination of four fabrics to construct this fabric, a 1¼-yard length of each of the four fabrics will be adequate to make four curtain panels. When using a stripe fabric for this design, allow the pattern width of the stripe selected to determine the strip size of this curtain. For a uniform look you may like to cut each strip the same size, or you may prefer a variety of strip widths. Allow the fabric to suggest the width. Try cutting a stencil from template material or cardboard, creating a window the finished size of the strip. Position the stencil over the fabric to preview the completed effect. This will suggest design modifications before you cut or sew the cloth together.

INSTRUCTIONS

1. Sew the strips together using either the rolled hem (Piecing on a Serger) or French Seams construction in the Glossary.

2. Finish the edges with a serged rolled hem or a straight sewn seam.

3. Attach ruffle or trimming, and finish header as suggested by Glossary methods.

3
JUMBO PLEATED VALANCE

Frame a bay window or give a standard window a subtle touch of mixed prints with this delightful window treatment. Use as few as one fabric for the front and liner, or three for this inverted pleat style. Join the curve section and backing, coordinating color and pattern with a favorite quilt.

Enlarge on a photocopier the jumbo pleated valance pattern provided on the next page to the desired length. Seam allowance will be ½". Using scraps of newspaper taped together, determine a pleasing width for your specific window opening. Pleat the paper pattern to the finished size for the window. This valance would be mounted over the window opening by the use of "hook-and-loop" tape, a type of Velcro™. The rough part of the tape, with the loops, is stapled or glued to the window frame. The fuzzy or hook part of the tape is stitched or glued to the curtain/valance backing. Hook-and-loop tape is strong and allows a firm yet smooth application. Needless to say, the application is simple and eliminates permanent nailing into the wall or molding.

MATERIALS

Valances are most commonly 15" to 18" in length. Allow ½" more than your length for seam allowance. Using the jumbo pleated valance paper pattern as a guide, determine the fabric width you require to cover the window. Remember to pleat the paper as you will your fabric to ensure the correct length. The width should conform to a fullness of 2 to 2½ times the window opening.

This valance requires a lining the full width of the fabric.

The valance photographed uses two fabrics on the front, fabric A and an accent fabric B. The accent fabric is positioned within the inverted pleat. The seam joining the two fabrics will be the pleat foldline.

IN ADDITION YOU WILL NEED:

Iron-on interfacing or iron-on lightweight batting

Matching sewing threads

Hook-and-loop tape

INSTRUCTIONS

1. Begin by creating your full-size newspaper pattern as previously instructed. The pleats will be created by folding under 2″ to 3″ to either side of a centerline. The pleat is constructed by a fold brought to the left of the pleat centerline, and a second fold brought to the right of the centerline. The outside fabric edges, including the foldlines, must be maintained evenly along the top edge of the valance.

2. Cut the fabric using your paper pattern as a guide, adding a ¼″ seam allowance around all sides.

3. Piece the sections together. To add body to the valance, fuse either iron-on interfacing or iron-on batting to the wrong side of the valance front. This will improve the drape as well as help withstand frequent laundering. Fuse the interfacing or batting to the lining side of the valance.

4. Insert a piping in the curved edge of the valance for additional definition or to provide an accent color. Follow the Glossary instructions for Making Piping.

5. With right sides of your fabric facing each other, sew the front of the valance to the lining layer. Seam around the sides and lower curved edge using a scant ¼″ seam allowance. Stitch on top of the piping seam as a guide.

6. Holding your scissor points at right angles to the seam, clip into the curves of the seams right up to the seamline. Cut across the corners as well. Reverse the valance and press. Topstitch in the ditch in matching thread ⅛″ from the piping edge. This will prevent the seam from rolling and will provide a crisp edge.

7. Pleat the valance, bringing the arrow lines to the dotted line. Sew over the top of the pleat down ½″ from the top edge. A hand-sewn or machine-stitched bar tack will secure the lower edge of the pleat. At the valance edge, turn the top ¼″ seam allowances in toward each other. Trim excess batting remaining in the top edge. Stitch the front and the lining together with matching thread.

8. Sew the hook-and-loop tape at least ½″ lower than the top edge. Glue or staple the hook-and-loop tape to the window frame. Mount the valance to the tape.

JUMBO PLEATED VALANCE PATTERN

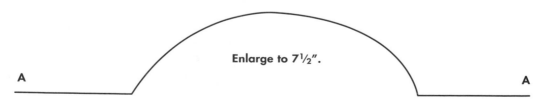

Enlarge to 7½″.

A   A

4

SAWTOOTH-BORDERED
CURTAINS

This design will coordinate many geometric quilt patterns with your curtain treatment. Use one print for the triangles or mix scraps from your favorite stockpile of odds and ends. Begin by measuring your window and determining the curtain length you require. If you decide that a 63″ length, slightly below the windowsill, is the look you like, use the 3″ finished triangle template for the pattern. The 3″ triangle will divide into the 63″ length evenly, a total of 21 triangles. If your curtain measurement yields an even number you can use the 4″ or 2″ template provided. My example will be using the 3″ size with a curtain length of 63″.

The valance in this project is attached to the curtain top. I stitched two parallel lines that created a header for the rod insertion. This is a simple method of construction and can be applied to other treatments in addition to this basic design.

MATERIALS

Using your window measurements to calculate yardage, you will need twice the window width for adequate fullness for your curtains. The length of the curtains is determined by adding several measurements. Start with the finished curtain length and add 4½″ for the header and 3½″ for the lower hem. If the fabric is 45" wide you may find it convenient to use this width for each curtain panel, assuming your window will use two panels per window opening. For windows up to 45" in width, panels utilizing the full fabric width are convenient to make and pleasingly full. Add together the total length of each unfinished panel, including valance sections, for the overall purchase requirement. Sanforized fabrics are guaranteed against shrinkage of more than 1%; this translates into an accepted shrinkage amount of up to ½" per yard. For this reason, prewash cotton fabric that will see frequent laundering, and allow some additional yardage in case of shrinkage before making the curtains.

Allow ½ yard for the patchwork triangles in this design for each single-sized window treatment. Additionally, whenever attaching a patchwork geometric curtain border, always line it too.

IN ADDITION YOU WILL NEED:

1 yard per curtain of cotton print or solid for triangles

1 yard per curtain of cotton print or solid for piping

8½ yards of ⅛" cording per curtain

Shirring tape

Matching sewing threads

INSTRUCTIONS

1. A 63"-length curtain will require twenty-one 3" triangles for a center front border. The width of the curtain panel is one fabric width of 44". Use a sawtooth edge for the valance as well as the lower panel border. This will require two lengths, or 88". Twenty-nine 3" triangles will finish to a length of 87". For simplicity's sake, sew twenty-nine triangles together to yield an 87" length; trim the panel to conform to the border length.

Refer to Gridding Lines and Right-Angle Triangles in the Glossary. The grid used for a 3" finished triangle will be 3⅞". Sew the triangle units as shown in the Glossary and assemble into the border length needed.

2. Attach the triangle borders to the inside of each panel. Maintain the darker printed triangle fabric on the outside edge with the basic fabric triangle in line with the body of the curtain.

3. Construct piping for the curtain. Refer to Making Piping in the Glossary for specific instructions.

4. Attach piping to the sawtooth edge on the curtain as well as the valance.

5. Finish the outside curtain edges with a ¼" hem. Refer to Hemming a Curtain in the Glossary.

6. Construct a lining from your basic fabric the length of the border unit and the border width plus ½" seam allowance. See Lining a Curtain and Preparing the Header in the Glossary. Sew the lining to the piping edge.

7. Turn the lining to the wrong side. Turn the lining raw edge under, meeting the seam. Fold the seam flat on the sewing machine bed, with the curtain panel to the left side as you work. Zigzag the seams flat with a matching color thread.

When constructing valances it is easier to line the entire valance straight across than it is to make two panels. Cut a lining the same dimensions as the valance. Sew the sides and lower edges to the finished valance with right sides facing each other. Clip the corners before reversing the valance. Then reverse and press. Position the valance's right side facing the curtain top's wrong side. Sew along the top edge. Flip the valance to the curtain's right side and press flat. Sew a 1½" seam along the top edge, and a second seam going through all the layers 3″ from the top edge, creating a casing, or rod pocket.

8. Sew shirring tape over the two casing seams to create even gathering, following the instructions in Installing Pleater or Shirring Tape in the Glossary. This is optional and can be eliminated if the fabric is sufficiently heavy to give a crisp and even fullness.

TRIANGLE TEMPLATE (MULTIPLE SIZES)

The dotted lines are for two-inch, three-inch, and four-inch full-size, finished triangles. The solid lines indicate the ¼-inch seam allowance required for piecing.

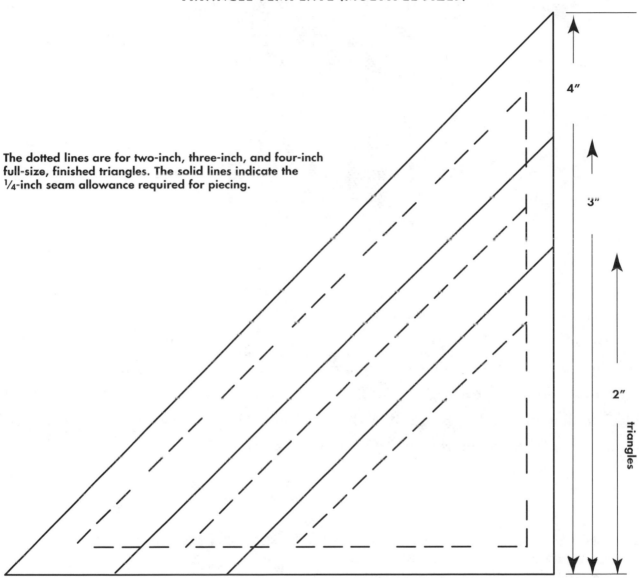

4″

3″

2″

triangles

5
BRODERIE PERSE CURTAINS

An old quilting technique inspired these simple and charming curtains. I selected a neutral background fabric that would complement the variety of colors in the appliqués. Nature demonstrates that green works with every color in the rainbow, and I believe this principle is as valid in quilting as in nature. In addition to my basic yardage I purchased a decorator print that had large floral motifs. Select a floral that has a dark brown or black outline to each flower or leaf. A 100% cotton will be the easiest fabric to work with. One yard of floral was more than sufficient for two curtains sets.

MATERIALS

Determine the curtain length you require, and add 6½" for hems, when using a conventional sewing machine. With a serger or overlock machine, use a rolled hem for the lower edge and save 3¼" per panel. The curtain width should be twice the window width for sufficient fullness. (Curtain directions frequently suggest 2½ times the fullness of the window, but the decorative treatment in this design would be lost with that much fabric.) The valance is a standard 15" in length, and twice the window width as well.

IN ADDITION YOU WILL NEED:

Large floral decorator print fabric for the appliqué

Wonder-Under™ fusible webbing

Shirring tape

Tear-away fabric stabilizer

Matching sewing threads

INSTRUCTIONS

1. Cut each curtain panel and hem the side seams. Using the directions for measuring and sewing a header in Lining a Curtain and Preparing the Header in the Glossary, complete the top edge. Repeat this method for the hem.

2. Follow the manufacturer's directions and apply Wonder-Under to the floral areas you wish to use. It would be wasteful to fuse the entire yard of floral; fuse only the flowers selected for your design.

3. If the curtain fabric has lines for reference, position the flowers in a pleasing manner along the lower and inside edge of the curtain. When using an unlined print, draw a line with an air-dry or a wash-out marking pen to ensure accurate placement. It is not necessary to make each panel symmetrical by repeating the same motif for all panels. Since the appliqués are cut from the same fabric, their uniformity of color and design blend the overall effect together.

4. Complete the curtain by sewing shirring tape beneath the rod casing seam, following the instructions given in Installing Pleater or Shirring Tape in the Glossary. The sample uses diamond tape that gives a very pleasing effect.

5. Cut the valance 18½″ in length and twice the window width. Hem the side edges with a 1″ seam. Using scallop guide A provided, mark the lower edge of the valance. Bind the lower edge if

the fabric is sufficiently firm. Prepare the header as shown in Lining a Curtain and Preparing the Header in the Glossary.

When working with quilting-weight fabric, pipe the lower edge and line the valance for added sufficient body. Refer to the Glossary for these instructions. You may prefer fusing interfacing onto the valance when using a very soft fabric. The piping gives a crisp finish as well as added drape to the project. When lining, turn the top raw edges in to meet each other, stitching with a ¼″ seam to finish. Leave 3″ unstitched along the top sides for a casing opening. Sew the standard 1½″ and 3″ seam lines for the casing.

6. Once the appliqués have been fused to the background curtain they will require stitching for durablity. It is not necessary to use a satin stitch to reinforce the flowers. Select a decorative stitch such as a buttonhole or featherstitch for this purpose. Practice with a sample of cloth, adjusting stitch length as well as width before sewing directly on the curtain. Sample thread colors, however; since the floral appliqués were outlined with a black line, you may be able to limit the thread color to black. Lighten the tension on the needle approximately two settings to create a more attractive stitch formation on the right side of the cloth. Most important use a tear-away stabilizer such as Stitch-N-Tear™, under the background fabric to eliminate puckering.

SCALLOP PATTERN A

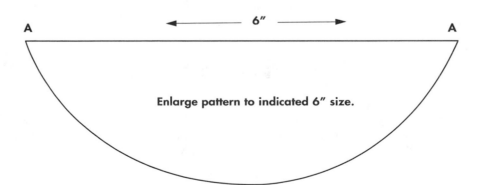

A ← 6″ → A

Enlarge pattern to indicated 6″ size.

6
DELPH HOUSE APPLIQUÉ CURTAINS

These curtains will offer an opportunity to play in your scrap pile of calico print and experiment with some of the decorative stitches on your sewing machine. The appliqué method used is an exciting new technique that eliminates a fusible bond product. One advantage is that it allows you to cut away the underlay fabrics. As the sun comes through the curtains you will not see unsightly levels of fabric upon fabric.

MATERIALS

Assorted cotton prints and solids for the house appliqués: a total of no less than ¼ yard of each of three fabrics, light, medium, and dark in value.

ThreadFuse™

Matching machine embroidery thread

Freezer paper

Indelible fine-line marking pen

Spray starch

INSTRUCTIONS

1. As in preceding curtain designs, begin by constructing the curtain panels twice the window width. Finish the side seams, lower hem, and headers. Refer to Hemming a Curtain and Lining a Curtain and Preparing the Header in the Glossary for more detailed instructions.

2. The instructions for Layered Machine Appliqué used in this design are presented in the Glossary. Trace the house pattern (next page) onto the coated side of a sheet of freezer paper. Use an indelible fine-line pen specifically made for marking plastic, wood, or glass, readily available in stationery or art-supply stores. One such pen is called Sharpie™ and is sold throughout the United States at a modest cost. Marking on the coated side will ensure that the design does not reverse. While this problem is not a consideration with our small symetrical house pattern, it can be a factor in many appliqué designs. Cut the freezer paper drawing at least 2″ beyond the sketch, and iron the paper to the wrong side of the curtain, pressing the coating against the fabric. Position the paper an even distance from the lower edge.

3. Prepare the appliqué fabric by cutting the fabric to be used at least 1″ larger than the overall design. Spray-starch the appliqué until the fabric is quite firm. This should require at least two passes of starch, one on the right side and another on the wrong side of the fabric.

4. Fill a bobbin with ThreadFuse™. Put the bobbin in your machine with a matching fabric thread in the needle.

5. Position the appliqué with the right side out on the right side of the curtain, overlapping the freezer paper guide. Check the position by holding the curtain up to a light source. Pin in place with flat-headed pins along an outer edge.

6. Working on the wrong side of the curtain, with a stitch length of 10 stitches per inch or 3mm, straight-stitch on the lines of the freezer paper pattern. ThreadFuse will be outlining the design on the right side of the appliqué fabric.

7. Remove the ThreadFuse from the bobbin and replace it with thread matching the needle thread color. Set your machine for a satin stitch,

referring to the owner's manual. The tension should be two settings lighter than normally used for construction sewing. This allows the stitching to lie attractively on the surface of the cloth. Satin-stitch over the ThreadFuse.

8. Using embroidery scissors or appliqué scissors, trim away the excess fabric from the edges of the satin stitching. To ensure a clean cut, hold your scissors with your palm up and the lower scissor blade against the stitching. If you are right-handed, work in a clockwise motion; left-handed operators should trim counterclockwise. With sharp scissors, barely open the tips of your shears and glide, trimming the fabric from the seam edge. Do not use a cutting motion as this could result in snipping the background fabric. The starched fabric will be an aid in trimming and will prevent the appliqués from puckering when they are against the feeddogs of the sewing machine in the first step of this technique. Starching is important, so do not neglect this step.

9. Appliqué the larger house sections, then complete the design by adding the small window and door sections. A ¾″-wide strip was added to the lower edge directly under the appliqués. This will straighten up any lower edges in the event your houses are not precisely positioned.

10. With machine embroidery thread, add an assortment of decorative stitches, roof lines, and interior design elements. Use a scrap of cloth with freezer paper or another stabilizer to try stitches before adding them to the curtain front.

11. Iron the appliqués, following the directions on the ThreadFuse package. The fusing agent on the thread will melt inside the satin stitching with pressing. This will reinforce the satin stitching and provide sufficient strength to the seam to allow you to cut away the layers.

12. Pull the freezer paper away from the curtain back.

13. With small embroidery scissors or appliqué scissors trim out the curtain fabric from behind the appliqués. Insert the scissor tip first to cut a small opening. Rest the tip along the satin stitching and carefully cut away all the layers.

DELPH HOUSE PATTERN

Half-size pattern

COUNTRY HEART PATTERN

7

COUNTRY HEART
VALANCE

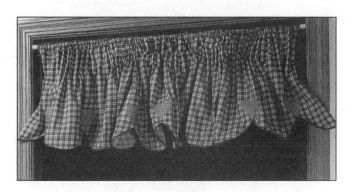

This valance complements the preceding Delph House curtains, and its construction is applicable to many designs.

MATERIALS

Cut the valance width required 2 to 2½ times the window size. The valance length is 18″ to the lowest scallop point.

INSTRUCTIONS

1. Complete the header following the Glossary directions for Lining a Curtain and Preparing the Header in the Glossary.

2. You can use Dritz™ Iron–on 4″ Pleater Tape for an even shirred finish, as in the valance shown. This is an excellent option when you wish to avoid stitching lines showing on the right side.

3. Complete the lower edges with a bias binding application. Since the edge is curved, the bias is required to conform to the rounded shape and lie flat. Refer to Binding by Machine in the Glossary.

Use a fusible bonding application, such as Wonder-Under™, for the hearts (pattern on page 16) or use the ThreadFuse™ method detailed in Layered Machine Appliqué in the Glossary.

8

PIECED TULIP CURTAIN

This design will help brighten any bedroom or kitchen with the addition of pieced and appliquéd flowers. Use an assortment of colors in the flowers, or maintain one color and vary prints.

MATERIALS

You can cut a 4½" section across the curtain width, and use this fabric for piecing the flowers. Cut the panel above the completed hem, so you can reattach this section and eliminate hemming the lower edge.

IN ADDITION YOU WILL NEED:

Assorted ⅛-yard lengths of red for the tulips

¼ yard of accent color for the flower centers

¼ yard of green solid for stems

¼ yard of green print for leaves

Wonder-Under™ fusible webbing

½ yard of cotton print or solid for lining the pieced insert

Tear-away fabric stabilizer

Matching sewing threads

INSTRUCTIONS

1. As for the Broderie Perse and Delph House curtain designs featured on pages 12 and 14, begin with the construction of the curtain. The curtains should be twice the fullness of the window opening. The length will be the finished size required plus the header and hem requirements. Refer to Lining a Curtain and Preparing the Header or Installing Pleater or Shirring Tape in the Glossary to determine the appropriate fabric requirement. Add 3½″ hems to the finished length and refer to the Glossary for Hemming a Curtain.

Once the fabric is cut for each curtain panel, begin the curtain construction by finishing the side edges. Fold a double hem of 1″ and topstitch this along the hem edge with matching thread. Complete the header, referring to the Glossary.

2. Determine the number of tulips you will need to insert in each curtain section. Select a number that is slightly less than the overall width of the curtain, and fill in the patchwork insert with curtain fabric at each outside edge to adjust the width.

3. Each tulip has six 1″ triangles of the main flower color sewn to the background print. Refer to the flower diagram. Total the number of right-angle triangles you will need for each panel and grid off for the triangle construction.

Refer to Gridding Lines and Right-Angle Triangles in the Glossary. Mark and sew the flower colors once you have gridded the background fabric. Since the curtain or background print is common to all the flowers, you can cut the background into grided sections to conform to the amount required.

4. Sew four pairs of triangles (that is, 4 squares of 2 triangles each) together to create the top row of the flower. Press. Cut a rectangle of the flower fabric, 2½″ × 4½″. Sew this across the first row of triangles. Refer to the diagram and sew a triangle pair (square) to either side of a 1½″ × 2½″ flower-fabric strip (a smaller rectangle). This will complete the final row of the flower; attach this to the first two sections. Using Wonder-Under fusible web, trace the center bud pattern provided on the next page and fuse the bud to the pieced flower. Repeat this process until all the flowers are completed. Flowers should be joined together with background strips cut to 1½″ × 4½″. Fill in with background fabric at the outside edges of the flowers to complete the panel. Sew the panel to the lower edge of the curtain, and join additional fabric for a lower hem edge. Cut a lining ½″ wider than this panel and attach it to the wrong side of the curtain,

FLOWER DIAGRAM

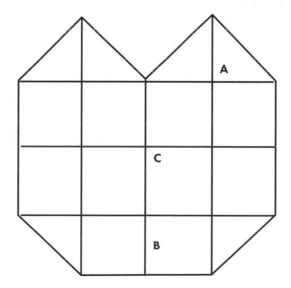

either at the same time as you attach the panel or by stitching in the ditch once the curtain assembly is complete.

5. The leaves and stems are attached to the hem section with the use of Wonder-Under. Follow the manufacturer's directions, and reinforce the edges with a decorative stitch. Remember to sta-

bilize your stitch area by positioning Stitch-N-Tear™, Tearaways™, or typing-weight paper under the wrong side of curtain during stitching. This will pull away once all the embroidery is completed. The curtain shown has a buttonhole stitch worked over the appliqué edges. This provides an old-fashioned look to the design and takes less time and thread than satin stitching.

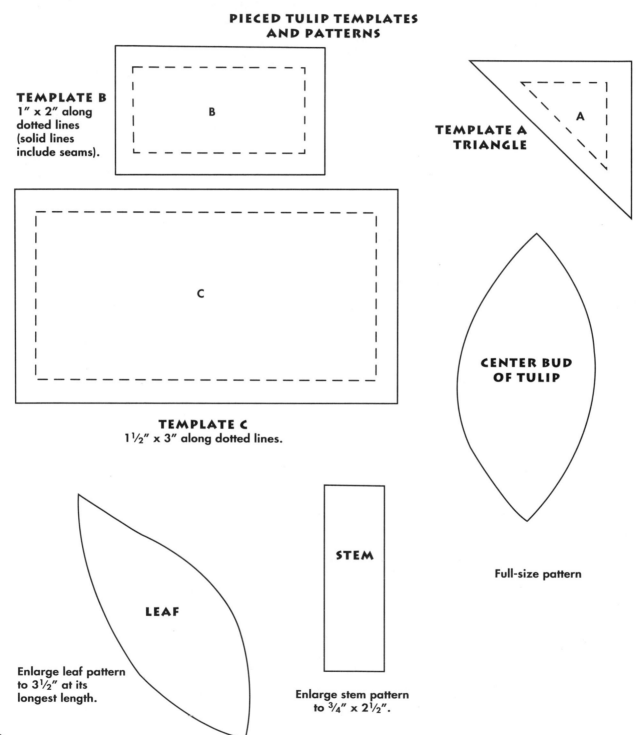

PIECED TULIP TEMPLATES AND PATTERNS

TEMPLATE B
1" x 2" along dotted lines (solid lines include seams).

B

TEMPLATE A TRIANGLE

A

C

TEMPLATE C
1½" x 3" along dotted lines.

CENTER BUD OF TULIP

Full-size pattern

LEAF

Enlarge leaf pattern to 3½" at its longest length.

STEM

Enlarge stem pattern to ¾" x 2½".

9
SEWING ROOM WINDOW TREATMENT

If you are fortunate enough to have a special room for sewing, I know that this design will tickle your fancy. For the past several years, fabric manufacturers have been producing a line of sewing-inspired prints. We purchase these treasures with enthusiasm and then rack our brains to find the right use for them. After stitching them together for quilt backings, sewing caddies, or vests, I think I have found the best use of all for these prints: curtains for the sewing room. Since the notion designs are available in quilting weight only, it will be necessary to line the curtains to prevent fading. With the variety of sewing prints growing every year, I suspect that the line has proved popular; therefore, while the prints shown might be discontinued when you read these instructions, something just as whimsical will be in the quilt shops. If you live in a remote area and simply cannot find sewing-motif fabric, I think you will agree that simple muslin will do the trick when combined with the appliqués and embellishments shown.

MATERIALS

Curtain yardage should be the length required with header and lower seam allowance. The yardage width is limited to 1½ times the window opening. This limited fullness allows for the appliqués to be a strong design element.

Ruffle fabric will be made from two prints: the background and an accent print. The ruffle will be twice the fullness of the curtain width.

IN ADDITION YOU WILL NEED:

Lining fabric in the same quantity as the background curtain print

Assorted solids for appliqués

Assorted buttons for appliqués

Wonder-Under™ fusible webbing

Matching sewing and embroidery threads

INSTRUCTIONS

1. Construct the curtain using the basic methods as given for Broderie Perse Curtains, page 12. For constructing the header refer to Lining a Curtain and Preparing the Header in the Glossary. The curtain side seams can be completed with a rolled hem on the serger.

2. Using the pattern provided, cut sufficient triangles for the ruffle area. The ruffle should be twice the curtain width. Piece the ruffle together. Cut a lining the same size and position it behind the ruffle. With a rolled hem, serge the two together along the side and lower edges. For conventional sewing machines, position the lining with right sides over the ruffle and stitch the two together using a $\frac{1}{4}''$ seam along the side and lower edges. Reverse and press.

3. Attach the ruffle to the curtain. Use the rolled hem attachment for a serger or bind the seam with a conventional sewing machine.

4. Fuse Wonder-Under to the wrong side of the appliqué fabrics. Using pinking shears, cut the

SEWING ROOM CURTAIN RUFFLE PATTERN

Add $\frac{1}{4}''$ seam allowance.

PIECING DIAGRAM

Enlarge pattern to indicated size. Add 3″ to long side of template B. Add 3″ to horizontal leg of triangle A.

appliqués into 2″ or 3″ squares. Remove the backing paper and fuse the appliqués in a random pattern to the curtain.

5. Stitch a button in the center of each appliqué to accent and anchor it in place. Refer to the owner's manual of your sewing machine for sewing a button in place. This is a wonderful opportunity to master this method.

SEWING ROOM SWAG AND JABOT

Since most quilters are serious about their craft I felt it most fitting to use this formal treatment to add stature to the sewing design.

MATERIALS

Measuring for the swag is important to determine the yardage you will require for the design. Though this design will be most conveniently installed with hook-and-loop tape, install a curtain rod at the window as a measurement aid. The swag is overlaid 1″ from the side edge of the jabot. The jabot measurement will be a constant for most window openings, but the swag will vary with the window size. With this in mind, drape a cord or string from the rod ends, with a center depth of 30″. Mark the end of the string with a felt-tip pen for your convenience. The depth includes seam allowance and header allowance. The length of the string will indicate the swag width required; add 1″ to your measurement for outside seam allowances. Piece different prints of fabric sections together until they are sufficient in size. Maintain the lengthwise fabric grain along the centerfront of the swag.

IN ADDITION YOU WILL NEED:

Matching length of lining fabric for the swag

1¾ yards of print or solid for the jabots

1¾ yards of lining fabric for the jabots. The jabot lining will be seen on the right side and should be an accent print or solid

Chalk for marking fabric

Matching sewing threads

Hook-and-loop tape

INSTRUCTIONS

1. Following the jabot diagram, cut two jabots from lining fabric and two from print fabric.

2. Sew the lining and outer print fabric together along the sides and lower edges. Clip across the corners and reverse. Press.

3. Turn the lining and outside fabric in toward

each other ½″ from the raw edge. Topstitch this hem.

4. Starting at the outer long side of the jabot, mark 3″ in from the side along the top edge. Using the pleat template, mark the pleat with chalk as indicated on the template. The arrows should point toward the long side of the jabot. Space 2″ intervals between pleats, and repeat marking until you have four pleats chalked in position at the top edge. Bring together the circles shown on the pleat template in working the pleats, folding toward the long outside edge of the jabot. Topstitch the pleats in place for a 2″ depth.

5. Use newspaper or shelving paper to prepare a pattern of the swag, as follows. The center depth of the swag will be 30″ and the width will be the measurement indicated by the string. The side seams of the swag will be very gradually decreased to a length of 28″. Along this side edge, measure 3″ from the lower edge and up the 28″ length. Mark pleat A at the position as indicated in the swag diagram. You will mark a total of three A pleats along the side edge, spacing a separation of 1″ between them. After the third A pleat, space 1″ and mark pleat B as indicated. Space another 1″ and complete your swag pattern with the full-size pattern provided for pleat C.

6. Cut the swag from the lining and outer fabric using your pattern as a guide.

7. Sew the swag outer fabric and lining together along their sides and lower edge. Clip the gradual curve and corner. Reverse and press.

8. Turn the top edges in toward each other and hem with a ½″ seam.

9. Starting with the lower pleats, bring the lines together, topstitching 2″ into the pleats to maintain their shape.

10. Overlay the swag 1″ from the side jabot edges and stitch through all the layers ½″ from the top edge.

11. The swag/jabot will be attached to the window with hook-and-loop tape. Sew the loop tape to the fabric backing, and staple the rough-side, or hook, tape to the window frame.

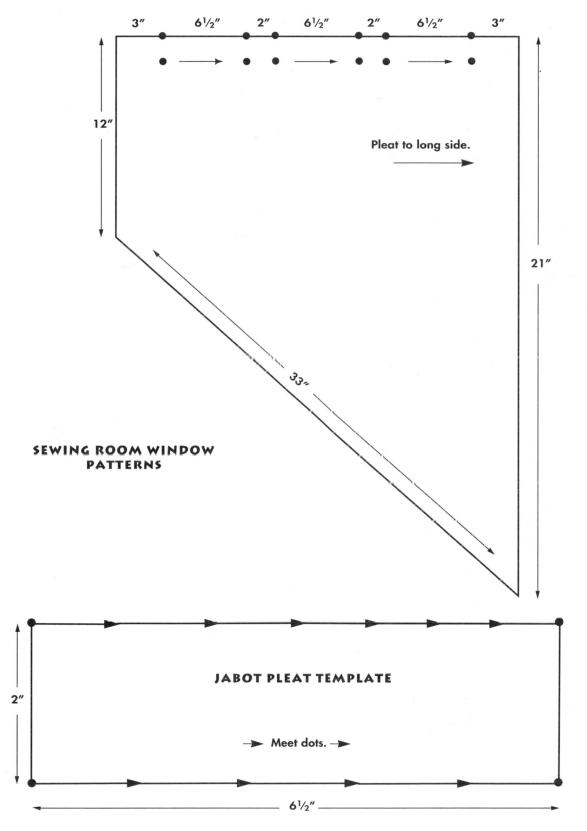

3"   6½"   2"   6½"   2"   6½"   3"

12"

Pleat to long side.

21"

33"

SEWING ROOM WINDOW PATTERNS

JABOT PLEAT TEMPLATE

2"

→ Meet dots. →

6½"

(continued next page)

SEWING ROOM PATTERNS

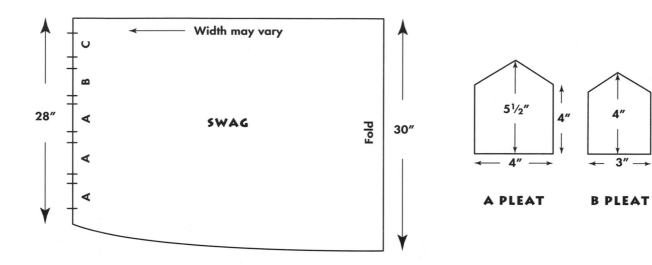

28"

C
B
A
A
A
A

Width may vary

SWAG

Fold

30"

5½" 4"

4"

4" 3"

4" 3½"

A PLEAT   **B PLEAT**

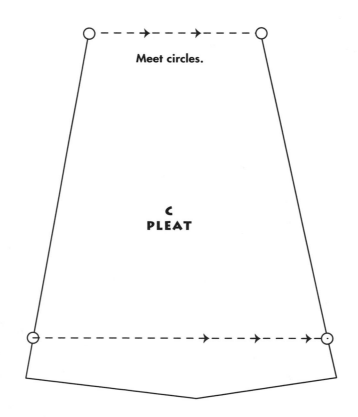

Meet circles.

**C
PLEAT**

PART TWO

QUILTED VALANCES

Quilted valances should be a standard companion for every bedquilt. With less than a yard, you will be able to give a coordinated look to an entire bedroom. It is not always necessary to make curtains from a fabric used in the quilt on the bed. Use muslin or a purchased sheer curtain for this purpose. Since hand quilting will not be seen at valance height, machine quilting will be most appropriate. Simplify pattern detail and scale, extracting as little as one motif from the matching quilt. Small prints will be unnoticeable three feet overhead as well and, in fact, their pattern will read as a solid. Appliqué by machine using Wonder-Under™, following the manufacturer's instructions, or with the ThreadFuse™ method presented in the Glossary (see Layered Machine Appliqué).

Basic directions for the valance designs presented in this section, as well as the many you will create on your own, have several considerations in common. First, the valances should finish to be approximately 18″ in length. The width is the size of the window opening, plus 6″ for rod return. The outer edges of the valance should turn at the rod ends and wrap at right angles to the wall to conceal the rod ends. Use batting in the valances to maintain their shape. Fusible batting made by Pellon™ was used for all the quilted valances shown in this book. It provides a firm valance that drapes well and will hold its shape with frequent laundering. The valances are lined, which prevents sunlight from showing through the patterns. This is aesthetically more appealing and prevents fading. Construct the valance front to 21″ and cut the lining 3½″ shorter than the front. Cut the batting the same size as the lining. Bring the outside fabric over the lining to create the header. Machine-quilt the valance and bind the lower edge. Attach a 2½″ or larger ruffle at the top edge or recess the rod pocket 2½″ down from the top edge. The trim or ruffle will cover the rod configuration behind the curtain.

The curtain rods of choice for the valance/curtain combination are the double-rodded hardware most commonly used for priscilla curtains or two spring rods used together. The front rod will carry the valance and the back rod will carry the matching curtain. It will not be necessary to install a mounting form for these designs.

To minimize time, the valance's tiebacks utilize machine piecing or appliqué. These accessories coordinate the valance with the curtain. Hook-and-loop tape will serve as the closure for the tiebacks, and can be a simple means of attaching the tieback or lower café curtain to the window.

10
BARGELLO VALANCE

This design is appropriate for more geometric, juvenile, or contemporary decorating. While it appears intricately pieced, this pattern can be accomplished with strip piecing in less than two hours.

MATERIALS

¼-yard lengths of each of five assorted prints and solids per valance. Vary the value of color within the selection, making certain to have at least one bright or light fabric for accent.

½ yard of cotton fabric for lining per valance
½ yard of batting per valance
Matching sewing threads
Plastic or cardboard for template

INSTRUCTIONS

1. Cut a 3½″ × 45″ strip across the width from all five of the fabrics selected.

2. Using ¼″ seam allowance, sew the strips together along their 45″ side in a pleasing order.

Once you have sewn all five fabrics, stitch the first and fifth fabrics together as well along their 45″ length. You should have a tube constructed at this point.

3. Using a hem roll, sleeve board, or cardboard roll from wrapping paper, iron the seam allowances open.

4. Lay the roll as flat as possible on your cutting board and, using a rotary cutter and ruler, cut the roll in segments. For this design, cut the segments of varying widths, from $1\frac{1}{2}$″ to $2\frac{1}{2}$″. The valance shown was cut into three different widths, $1\frac{1}{2}$″, $1\frac{3}{4}$″, and $2\frac{1}{2}$″.

5. Start at the center front of the valance for piecing. Open one $2\frac{1}{2}$″ band at one seam to make a flat segment. See color plate 8. I opened the seam between my blue print and my purple solid. Take two $1\frac{1}{2}$″-wide strips and open their seams one seam lower than the previous band—in the photograph, the seam between the blue and the yellow fabric.

6. Sew the $1\frac{1}{2}$″ segments to either side of the $2\frac{1}{2}$″ center front band. Press this unit flat.

7. Skipping to the next seam down (in plate 8, the yellow and green fabrics' seam), cut two bands $1\frac{3}{4}$″ in width. Match the seams carefully to the three-sectioned unit, and attach these bands on either side of center front. Press this assembled section flat.

8. From the pieced tube cut two bands $2\frac{1}{2}$″ wide, and open their seams to form flat bands, one seam below the previous color pair. This is green and rose in plate 8. Sew these bands to either side of the valance center front. Press after attachment.

9. Continue to cut a variety of strip widths from the tube one seam below the color combination used in the previous set and open them to flat

bands. With each attachment, match seams carefully, pinning and checking to prevent misplacing or inverting the band colors. Work in pairs of band size and color, attaching each to either side of the developing valance. Press after each addition to keep the work accurate as well as neat during construction. Sew a sufficient number of sections together until the valance is the desired width for the window opening, plus a rod return of 6″.

10. Make a curve template from plastic or cardboard using the Bargello scallop pattern provided. Position the curve template with the narrow V shape under the valance center front, and mark the lower edge of the valance. Add a $\frac{1}{4}$″ seam allowance to the marked line, and trim off the excess fabric.

11. Cut the valance lining and batting the same size as the front. From the lining fabric cut a $4\frac{1}{2}$″ wide band the same width as the valance.

12. Pin the batting behind the valance. If you are using fusible fleece, fuse the batting to the wrong side of the valance front. The $4\frac{1}{2}$″ band will be used as a rod pocket. Baste this strip to the top edge of the batting. With right sides facing each other, pin the valance front to the lining. Sew across the top edge. Maintain a 9″ opening on one side down from the top edge; stitch the remainder of that side, across the lower edge, and up the last side to 4″ from the top edge. Clip into points and across angles, and trim excess batting from the seam allowances. Reverse the valance through the 9″ opening.

13. Turn the seam allowance on each short side of the valance, raw edges in, and sew. Maintain an opening in this side section for the rod pocket. Press the valance flat.

14. Begin by sewing $\frac{1}{4}$″ in from the edge around the top, sides, and lower edge to give a sharp definition to the valance shape.

15. One inch from the top edge, sew across the valance width in a matching thread.

16. Three inches from the top edge, sew the lower seamline to complete the rod pocket.

17. Since fusible fleece was used in the construction of the valance shown, quilting the valance was limited to echo or outline quilting 1″ up from the lower edge. When using batting that does not have a fusible agent, it is advisible to add additional quilting for every 5″ of surface area.

BARGELLO SCALLOP

A B C

Enlarge scallop pattern to following recommended size:

7″ from point A to point B
2″ from point B to point C

SPIRAL PATCHWORK TIEBACKS

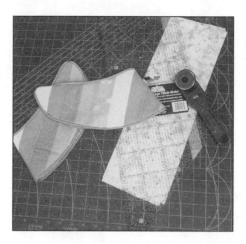

The coordinating curtain tier utilizes one print used in the Bargello Valance, and is constructed using the rolled hem (see Piecing on a Serger) and header (see Lining a Curtain and Preparing the Header) methods explained in the Glossary.

MATERIALS

5, 2″ × 44″ strips of fabric, 1 from each of the five fabrics used in the Bargello Valance

Plastic or cardboard for template

½ yard of polyester batting per valance

5 yards of piping (2½ yards per tieback)

Hook-and-loop tape

Matching threads

INSTRUCTIONS

1. Sew the strips of fabric together along their 44″ length using a ¼″ seam allowance. Construct Spiral Patchwork, according to the specific instructions in the Glossary.

2. Using the Colonial Rose Tieback pattern provided on page 38, make a template to cut two tiebacks per window from the spiral patchwork

you made. Cut two lining and batting units using the same template.

3. Pin or fuse the batting on the wrong side of the tieback front.

4. Construct piping for the tieback edge, referring to Making Piping in the Glossary. Each pair

of tiebacks will require 2½ yards of piping. Align the raw edge of the piping with the raw edge of the tieback front, and with the aid of the zipper foot for your sewing machine, stitch the piping around the edge. Overlap the piping at the outside curved edges to reduce bulk in the seams.

5. Position the tieback front over the backing, and sew in the piping seamline to join the layers together. Leave at least a 6″ opening along the lower edge of the tieback for reversing. Clip into the concave curve of the tieback edge before turning. Reverse. Hand-stitch the opening closed.

6. Use hook-and-loop tape to hold the ends together when positioning on the window.

11
COLONIAL ROSE VALANCE

This valance design should harmonize with numerous traditional appliquéd quilt patterns. The valance colors are not true to nature but demonstrate that you are free to select the color palette solely upon the quilt or room colors.

MATERIALS

5/8 yard of muslin or background fabric per valance

½ yard of lining fabric per valance

½ yard of polyester batting per valance

⅛ yard of each of three cotton prints for

appliquéd leaves, stems, and flowers

2 yards of 1½″ bias binding made from an appliqué fabric or background muslin

Matching sewing threads

Freezer paper

INSTRUCTIONS

1. Using a dark marking pen, trace the design provided on page 36 onto tracing paper. Position the design under the background fabric, center- ing the fabric over the full flower. The design should be approximately 3″ from the lower edge. Using a soft pencil or wash-out marking pen (air-dry markers may fade too quickly for this project), trace the design onto the fabric front. This will serve as a guide when you position the appliqués.

2. Trace the design over freezer paper to prepare the appliqués. Carefully cut the drawn motifs out from the freezer paper, and press the coated or shiny side of the freezer paper motifs to the wrong side of the appliqué fabric. Iron these in place. Cut the shapes out from the fabric, $\frac{1}{4}''$ beyond the paper edges. With a needle and thread, baste the excess seam allowance over the paper edge. When turning a curve, clip up to the paper edge. Baste the seam allowance over the paper, keeping the thread knots on the outside of the appliqués. After basting, press the appliqués with an iron.

3. Position the stem appliqués over the background using the outline as a guide. (Use ordinary sewing thread in matching colors and blindstitch the appliqué edges to the background. Work with a single thread. If you are right-handed, sew in a counterclockwise direction. If you are left-handed, work clockwise. Let the needle enter at the top fold of the appliqué. As the needle leaves the top edge of the appliqué, place its tip into the background fabric behind and in line with the short stitch just made in the appliqué. On the wrong side of the background, turn the needle to reenter the cloth ahead and in the tip of the appliqué to begin repeating this stitch formation. The stitch separation should not exceed $\frac{1}{4}''$ for strength). Position the bud tip in place, then lap the leaves over this small bud section. Complete the design with the leaves, center rose, and circle. Before sandwiching the layers of backing and batting, remove the freezer paper within the layers.

4. To do this, use small embroidery scissors to cut a small hole in the backing layer behind the

appliqués. Insert the scissors in this opening and carefully cut away the layers of fabric beneath the appliqués. Remove the basting stitches in the appliqué and peel out the freezer paper.

5. Use scallop pattern A provided on page 13 to mark the valance edge. Begin marking a center scallop in the center front of the valance. Add an equal number of scallops to either side of the valance until the full width is marked. Cut the fabric on the marked lines. The length of the valance front should be 21". Cut the lining and batting 3" less than the valance front.

6. Refer to Gridding Quilting Lines and Right-Angle Triangles in the Glossary. Mark a grid on the valance front.

7. Layer the batting and the lining behind the front, and safety-pin in place between the marked grid lines. Using matching sewing thread, machine-quilt the layers together.

8. Use an overlock stitch on the serger, or machine-sew the raw edges on the sides together to finish the side edges. Turn the seamed side edges over and topstitch in place. Refer to Binding by Machine in the Glossary, to create bias binding for completing the curved edges. Clip into the scallop corners before turning the bias to the wrong side to finish with hand or machine stitching.

9. Bring the extended $3\frac{1}{2}''$ of the valance top over to the backing to construct the header/rod pocket. Turn over a $\frac{1}{4}''$ seam allowance along the header band or overlock this edge using a serger. Machine-stitch the header to the valance $3\frac{1}{4}''$ from the top edge, stitching through all the layers. Complete the rod pocket by stitching a parallel row 2" down from the top edge for a common priscilla curtain-rod pocket. Modify this opening size for wider rods.

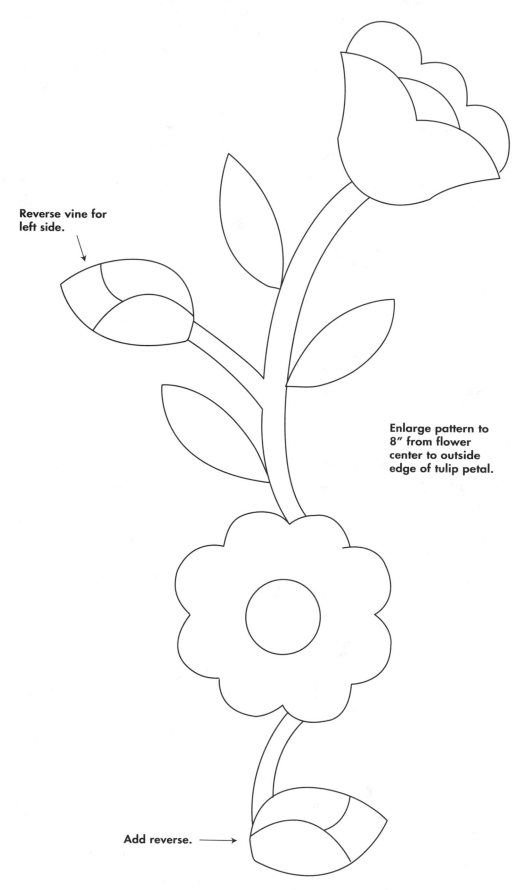

Reverse vine for left side.

Enlarge pattern to 8" from flower center to outside edge of tulip petal.

Add reverse.

COLONIAL ROSE TIEBACKS

MATERIALS

¼ yard of background fabric for each pair of tiebacks

¼ yard of lining fabric for each pair

¼ yard of batting for each pair

Small quantity of cotton scraps for appliqués

Freezer paper

Matching sewing threads

Marker pen

Tracing paper

Pencil or washout marking pen

ThreadFuse or Wonder-Under (optional)

INSTRUCTIONS

1. Trace the pattern provided on page 38 for the tieback onto the background fabric. Handling during construction will be easier if you do not cut out the tiebacks, but only outline their configuration as a guide.

2. Using a dark marker, trace the rose appliqué design on tracing paper. Position the drawing under the background fabric, and mark the design on the background with a light pencil line or a wash-out marking pen. Mark the pattern on only the right side of one tieback, and on the left side of the other tieback. These markings will be a placement guide for either Wonder-Under™ fusible bonding or attaching by hand.

3. To cut out the appliqués, follow the instructions in step 2 of the Colonial Rose Valance project, page 34. To attach the appliqués by hand, follow the instructions in step 3 of the Colonial Rose Valance project. If you prefer, you may use a machine-appliqué method of construction using ThreadFuse™ (outlined in Layered Machine Appliqué in the Glossary) or Wonder-Under.

4. With the appliqué completed, lay the batting and the lining fabric behind the tieback background fabric. Pin the layers and cut through all the layers.

5. Position the batting behind the front and safety-pin in place, keeping the pins away from the seam allowance. Lay the lining over the front with right sides facing each other, and sew the layers together using a ¼″ seam allowance. Leave an opening along the lower edge of the tieback. Refer to the tieback pattern for the position of the opening.

6. Trim the batting from the seam allowance, and clip into the concave side of the curve before turning the tieback right side out. Reverse and press.

7. Baste the opening closed. Topstitch ¼″ in around the entire tieback. This stitching should secure the opening as well as provide a crisp finish to the tieback.

8. Use hook-and-loop tape to close the tieback and secure it to the window.

COLONIAL ROSE TIEBACK PATTERN

Enlarge tieback pattern to 9¹/2" from foldline to outside of curved edge.

—Cut two—

Place on fold.

12

RIBBONED TULIP VALANCE

This valance is a great favorite, combining two popular motifs, tulips and bows. Use a muslin background or a light print. In order to achieve the effect of turning ribbon, use two fabrics for the ribbon, a print and a solid. The sample photographed used hand appliqué; however, Wonder-Under™ or the ThreadFuse™ method (see Layered Machine Appliqué in the Glossary) for machine appliqué will also work up nicely.

MATERIALS

⅝ yard of muslin or background fabric per valance

½ yard of lining fabric per valance

½ yard of polyester batting per valance

⅛ yard of each of two ribbon fabrics, two tulip prints, and two greens for leaves

2 yards of 1½" bias binding made from an appliqué fabric or background muslin

Matching sewing threads

Freezer paper

INSTRUCTIONS

1. Using a dark marking pen, trace the ribboned tulip design provided onto tracing paper. Position the design under the background fabric, keeping the lower leaf 3″ from the lower edge. Use a soft pencil or a wash-out marking pen to trace the outline of the design onto the fabric front. This will serve as the placement for the appliqués.

2. Trace the design onto freezer paper. Follow the instructions for freezer paper appliqué as given in step 2 of the Colonial Rose Valance, page 34.

3. The solid ribbon segments should be placed on the background first, overlapped by the printed ribbon and bow appliqués. Blindstitch these in place, referring to the specific suggestions for hand-sewing appliqué in steps 3 and 4 of the Colonial Rose Valance, page 34. Complete the placement of the leaves, buds, and tulips in the order indicated by the design. Trim the excess fabrics from under the appliqués.

4. Using the scallop pattern A, on page 13, mark the valance edge. Center one scallop and mark the edge, working toward the outside. The length of the valance front will be 21″. Cut the batting and the lining 3½″ less in length. Mark a grid on the front, referring to Marking a Gridded Quilting Pattern in the Glossary for instructions.

5. Layer together the front, batting, and lining, trimmed to shape. Align the scallop edge, with the batting and lining shorter than the front on the top straight side. Safety-pin the layers together for machine quilting, positioning the pins out of the marked line paths. With matching thread, machine-quilt on the gridded lines.

6. Overlock or hem the side raw edges. Using self-made bias binding, bind the lower scallop edge, referring to Binding by Machine in the Glossary for instructions.

7. Bring the extended 3½″ of the valance front over the backing to construct the header/rod pocket. Turn over a ¼″ seam allowance along the header band or overlock this edge. Machine-stitch the header 3¼″ from the top. Sew a parallel row of stitching 2″ from the top edge to complete the pocket edge.

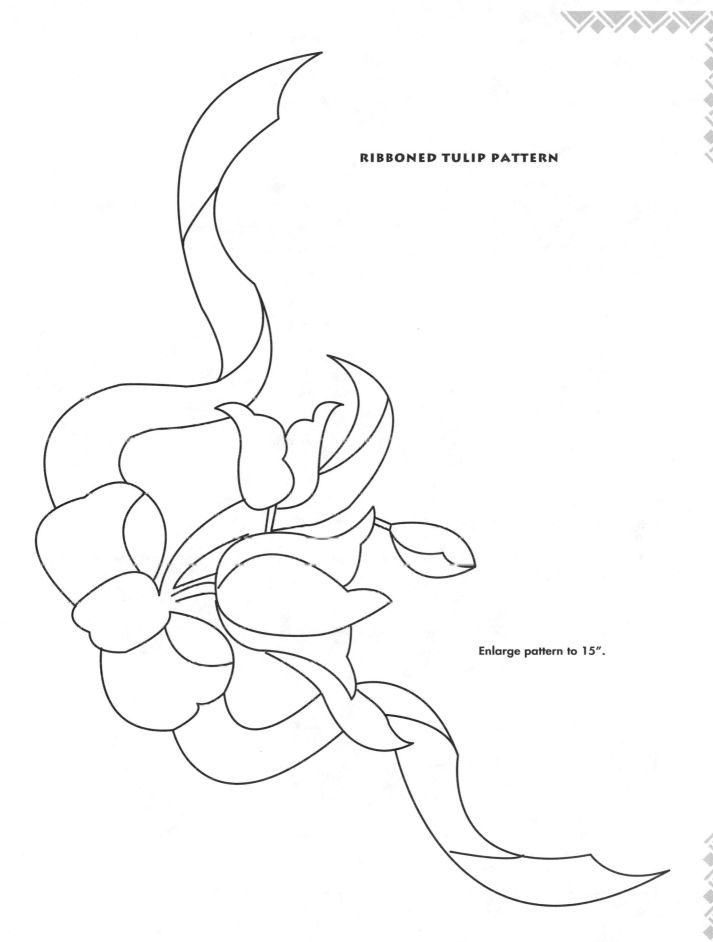

RIBBONED TULIP PATTERN

Enlarge pattern to 15".

41

TULIP BUD TIEBACKS

MATERIALS

¼ yard of background fabric for each pair of tiebacks

¼ yard of cotton lining fabric for each pair

¼ yard of batting for each pair

Small quantity of scrap calico for appliqués

Matching sewing threads

Freezer paper

Hook-and-loop tape

INSTRUCTIONS

1. Trace the tulip bud pattern for the tieback shape to the background fabric. It will be easier to do the appliqué if you do not cut out the small shapes until this stitching is completed.

2. Using a dark marker, trace the tulip bud appliqué design to paper. Position the paper under the background fabric, over the marked sections. Use a wash-out marker or a soft pencil and lightly outline the appliqués on the background fabric. This will serve as your appliqué placement guide.

3. Prepare the appliqués using the freezer paper and the blindstitch method given in steps 2, 3, and 4 of the Colonial Rose Valance instructions, page 34.

4. Remove the excess fabric from behind the appliqués. Cut the batting and the lining the same size as the tieback front. Pin the batting behind the front, and lay the two with right sides facing each other over the lining cotton. Sew a ¼″ seam through all layers, leaving a 4″ opening on the lower edge to reverse the tieback. Trim the excess batting, and clip into any curves. Reverse and press.

5. Baste the opening closed, and complete stitching ¼″ in around the outside shape.

6. Use hook-and-loop tape at the ends to join the tiebacks together and to attach the pair to the window for hanging.

TULIP BUD TIEBACK PATTERN

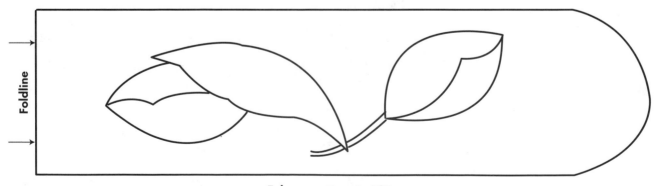

Enlarge pattern to 10″.

13
GRANDMOTHER'S FAN VALANCE

Fan quilts have enjoyed a constant popularity since their introduction in the latter part of the nineteenth century. Even without a fan quilt for the bed, this is a wonderful opportunity to add old-fashioned charm to a window. Determine the window opening and add 6" to this measurement for rod return and that is the size valance you need construct. Too much fullness will detract from the valance form, so maintain the window opening size for the valance width.

MATERIALS

⅝ yard of background print per valance

⅝ yard of cotton lining per valance

⅝ yard of polyester batting per valance

⅛ yard of each of eight assorted prints for fan segments

2 yards of 1½"-wide cotton eyelet trim

2½ yards of ¼" satin ribbon in each of two colors

Matching sewing threads

Plastic template material

Freezer paper

INSTRUCTIONS

1. Trace the fan valance pattern on plastic template material for convenience. The pattern contains a $\frac{1}{4}''$ seam allowance.

2. Mark three fan segments on each of seven print fabrics. Arrange one piece from each of the prints together in a pleasing arrangement and sew them together to form the lower fan unit.

3. Draw the quarter-circle fan valance pattern onto freezer paper. Omit the seam allowance on the curved side of the freezer paper. Cut one quarter circle of fabric for each fan. Pin the paper to the wrong side of the fabric wedge. Keep the coated side of the paper up and the straight sides of the paper and the fabric in line. Using a hot iron, gently press the fabric in the curved seam allowance over the glazed coating of the paper. This will enable you to iron the curved seam flat, eliminating the need to baste this seam allowance. Once the piece is securely pressed, gently peel away the paper from the seam. Position the quarter circle over the top seam allowance of the completed fans, and topstitch using a $\frac{1}{8}''$ seam.

4. Cut the background fabric the finished width the window requires (including the 6″ for rod returns) and add 1″ for seams. Lay the background fabric on a flat surface. Iron under a $\frac{1}{4}''$ seam allowance along the straight sides of the fans. Lay the fans out, ends touching one another, along the lower edge of the background

print. The curved edges should extend over the background edge. Topstitch the fans to the background. Trim the background fabric from behind the fans.

5. Cut batting and lining the same size as the front. Pin the batting behind the front of the valance.

6. With right sides facing each other, sew the layers together along the sides and lower edge of the valance. Leave the top open. Clip across the corners and into the curved seams before reversing. Reverse and press.

7. The measurement for this valance includes a $3\frac{1}{2}''$ header. Finish the top edge of the valance by overlocking with a serger or turning the seam allowances in to each other with a conventional sewing machine. Topstitch the sides and lower edge. Sew the eyelet to the fan edge, turning the trim's raw edges over themselves to finish.

8. Refer to Marking a Gridded Quilting Pattern in the Glossary and draw a 2″-wide grid over the surface of the valance background. Machine-quilt on the grid lines and in the fan seams.

9. Bring the top edge of the valance over to the back to create the header. Sew one seam 2″ from the top and a second row of stitching $3\frac{1}{2}''$ down from the top edge through all the layers. This will create the rod pocket.

GRANDMOTHER FAN VALANCE AND TIEBACK PATTERNS

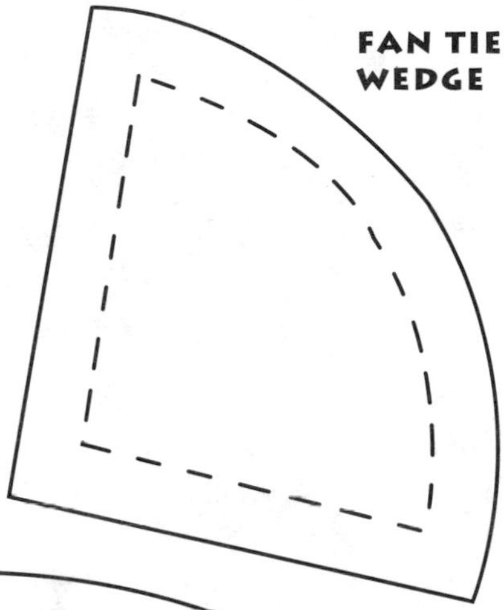

FAN TIEBACK WEDGE

Enlarge fan tieback wedge to 2" along straight dotted line.

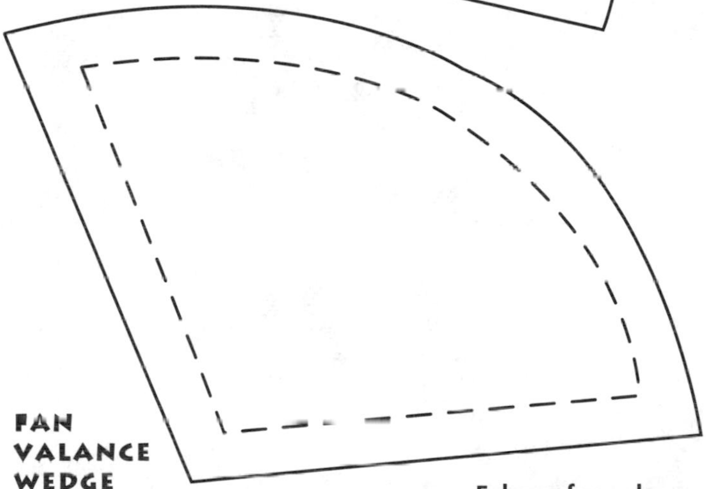

FAN VALANCE WEDGE

Enlarge fan valance wedge to 3" along dotted straight line.

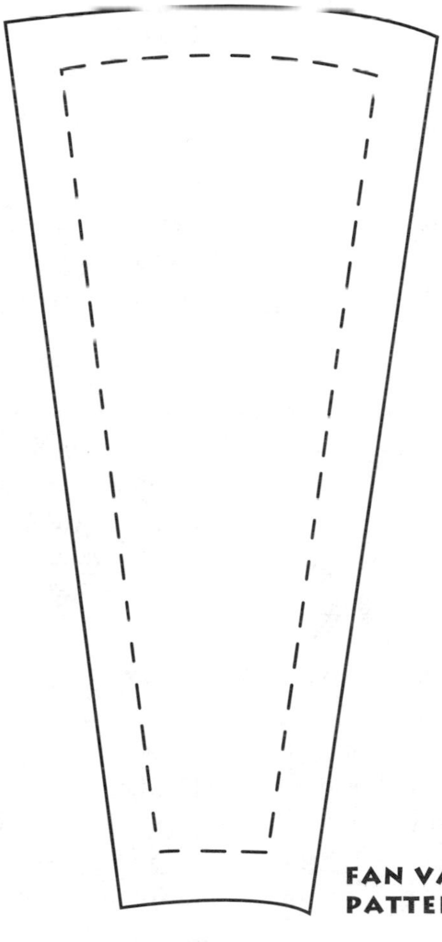

FAN VALANCE PATTERN

Enlarge fan valance to 4½" within dotted lines.

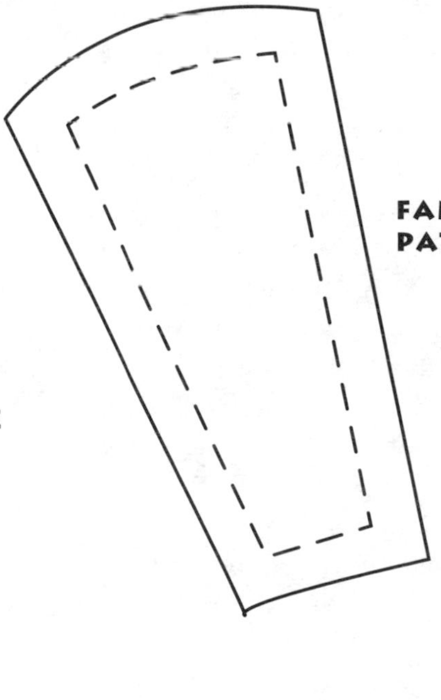

FAN TIEBACK PATTERN

Enlarge fan tieback pattern to 2¼" within dotted lines.

GRANDMOTHER'S FAN TIEBACKS

MATERIALS

¼ yard of background cotton print for each pair of tiebacks

¼ yard of cotton lining for each pair

¼ yard of batting for each pair

Small quantity of cotton print scraps for fan segments and quarter-circle segment

½ yard of 1¼"-wide cotton eyelet trim

Matching sewing threads

Plastic template material

Freezer paper

Hook-and-loop tape

INSTRUCTIONS

1. Trace the fan tieback pattern on plastic template material and cut six segments from an assortment of cotton fabric for each fan you require. Sew the six together using a ¼" seam allowance.

2. Trace the quarter-circle tieback pattern to freezer paper. Pin the paper to the wrong side of the fabric selected for this section with the coated side up. Cut the curved side ¼" larger than the paper. With a hot iron, press the excess seam allowance over the freezer paper's curved side. The seam allowance should stick to the wrong side of the fan as you press. Press the curve again sharply with the paper inside the layers. Gently remove the paper. Position the quarter circle over the seam allowance of the fan segments. Pin this in place and topstitch through all the layers. If you wish your stitching to be inconspicuous, use nylon monofilament thread in the needle. Stitch with a blindstitch or buttonhole stitch for appliquéing the quarter circle to the fan.

3. Cut batting and backing the same size as the completed fan. Position the batting behind the front and safety-pin in place. With the right side

of the lining facing the fan front, sew the two together leaving one straight side open. Clip into the curves before reversing. Turn and press with right side out. Turn the seams into each other and topstitch to close. Lay the eyelet behind the completed fan and stitch the top curve of the fan, going through to the eyelet layer to secure the trim.

4. Trace the tieback pattern to the fabric, and cut one front, one batting, and one lining. Position the batting behind the top layer, with the lining and front facing each other, right side to right side. Sew around all sides, leaving an opening about 4" on the top edge. Clip into curves, and trim any excess batting from the seam allowances. Reverse and press.

5. Fold the tieback in half to determine the placement of the accent fan. The fan's curve will be placed over the fold of the tieback. Take care to construct a right and a left tieback section (refer to the photograph). Topstitch the fan to the tieback.

6. Use hook-and-loop tape to secure the ends and to fix the tieback to the window.

14

SWEET STARS VALANCE

This valance reflects a basic technique of inserting a pieced quilt block into a valance design. The block used is 12″ in size. The top of the valance uses a 2½″ ruffle for a soft accent on an otherwise severe geometric motif. As always, the fabric used will make a design masculine, southwestern, country, or formal.

MATERIALS

⅝ yard of background print fabric per valance

⅝ yard of lining fabric per valance

⅝ yard of polyester batting per valance

¼ yard of each of four print fabrics for the patchwork star blocks

2 yards of 1½″ bias binding made from one of the print fabrics used in the star blocks

Matching sewing threads

Plastic template material

INSTRUCTIONS

1. Trace the triangles and square patterns on page 49 onto plastic template material adding a ¼″ seam allowance. Follow the block diagram also provided on the next page and refer to the photograph as a fabric selection guide. Sew the corner triangle A's together first. Sew one triangle B to either side of triangle C. Assemble the block by piecing the square D to a B/C section to create the center section of the star. The final assembly step is sewing two small triangle B's cut fromthe same fabric used for triangle C. This is the striped fabric shown in the valance photograph. Sew two of the light-colored B's to either side of a B/C starpoint section. Attach an outer triangle B to the outside of this section, and the outer top and lower sections of the star are completed. Repeat this assembly for the lower third of the block.

2. Cut four large triangles from the background fabric using template E. Sew these to each outside corner to turn the star on point and increase the block to its 12″ finished size.

3. Sew the three blocks together, and add two background fabric strips, both the same size, one to each side section of the valance. The added strips should bring the valance to its required width, including the rod return measurement of 6″. Add a band for the header at the top edge of the block assembly. Sew a 4″ strip to the bottom of the valance for the scallop edge. Using the scallop pattern A (on page 13), mark the lower edge. Mark the front for a 3″ grid, referring to Marking a Gridded Quilting Pattern in the Glossary for details. It is important to note that due to the seaming required for a pieced block valance, a print background fabric is recommended. This will help to reduce visiblity of the seams.

4. Cut the batting. Pin the batting and the lining behind the wrong side of the valance front. Quilt the layers on the grid lines.

5. Overlock the raw edges or turn them in toward each other and topstitch. Bind the curved edge with bias binding made from one of the star-block prints.

6. For a header, turn $3\frac{1}{2}$″ of the top edge over to the wrong side. Refer to Lining a Curtain and Preparing the Header in the Glossary for constructing a header.

7. From the background print, cut a strip 4″ wide whose length is at least twice the width of the valance. Fold this in half along the long side with right sides out and iron it. This strip will serve as the top ruffle for the valance. Gather the length of the strip to the finished width of the valance. Refer to New Options for Gathering Ruffles in the Glossary. Sew the ruffle to the valance top to complete the project.

SWEET STARS VALANCE DIAGRAM AND TIEBACK BLOCK PATTERN

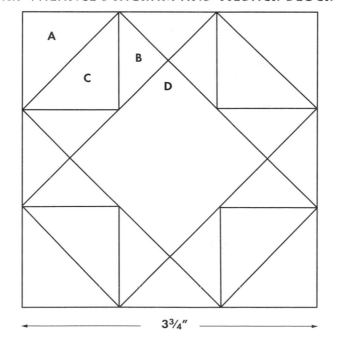

For tiebacks, enlarge block to indicated size.

3¾″

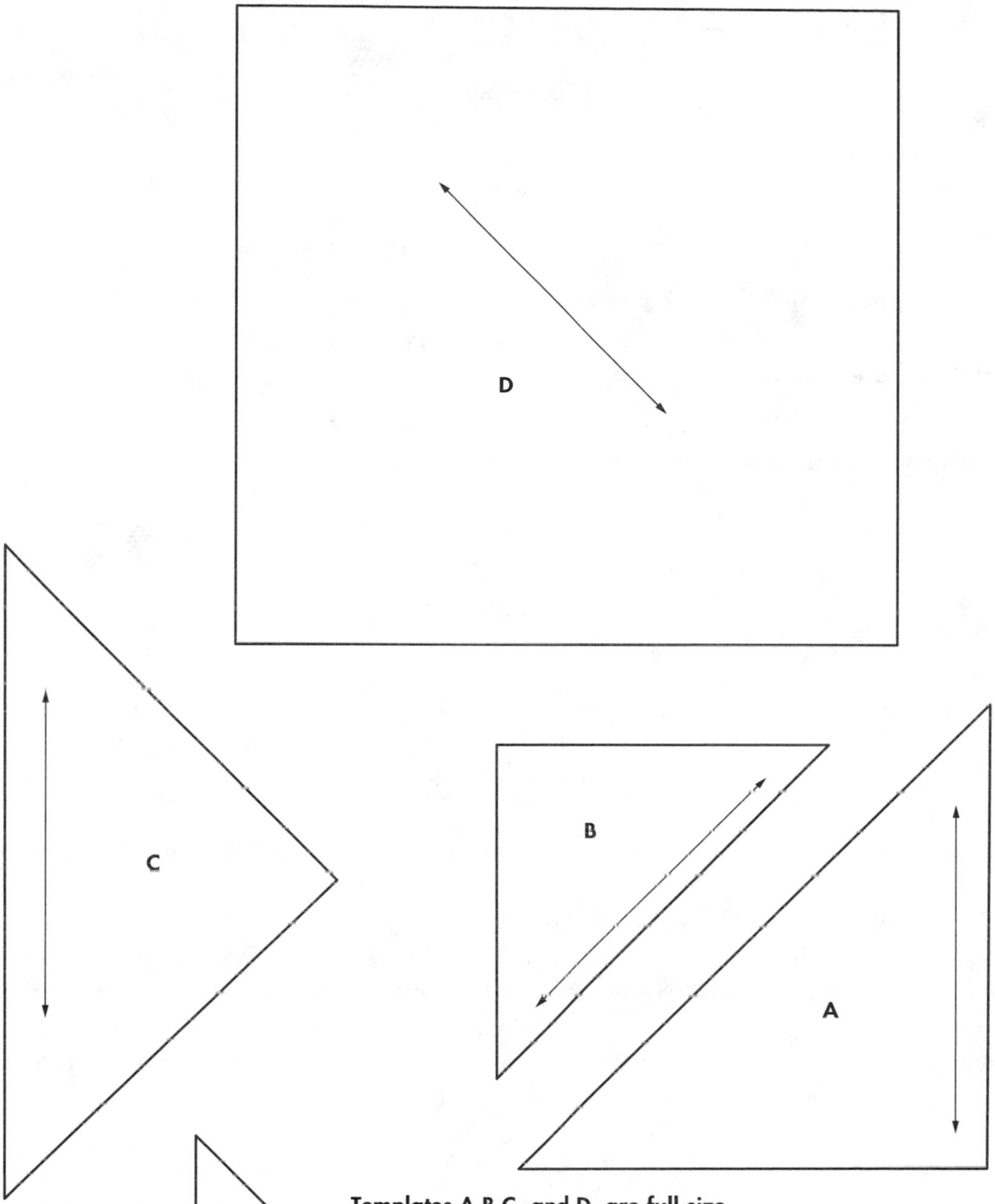

D

C

B

A

Templates A,B,C, and D are full size.
Add ¼" seam allowance.

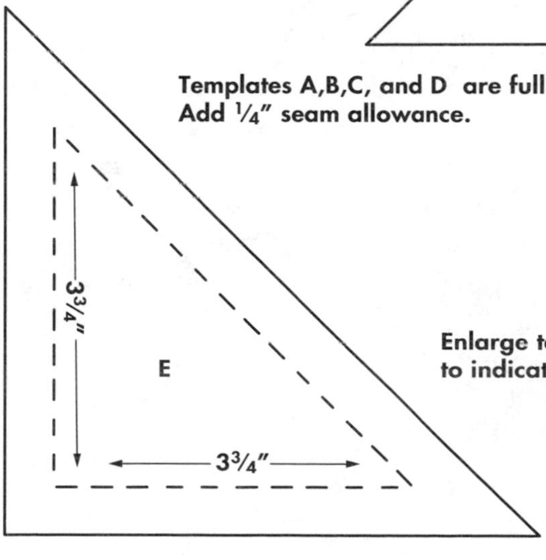

E

$3\frac{3}{4}$"

$3\frac{3}{4}$"

Enlarge template E
to indicated size.

SWEET STARS PATCHWORK TIEBACKS

MATERIALS

¼ yard of background fabric for each pair of tiebacks

¼ yard of lining fabric for each pair

¼ yard of batting for each pair

Small quantity of cotton scraps for miniature star block

2½ yards piping for edge

Matching sewing threads

Plastic template material

Hook-and-loop tape

INSTRUCTIONS

1. Trace the patterns for the miniature block (3¾") onto plastic template material. Follow the block-assembly instructions in step 1 of the Sweet Stars Valance, page 47, to construct the two miniature blocks. Press the blocks.

2. Use the Colonial Rose tieback pattern on page 37 to cut out two batting sections. As you work, make certain to construct batting for a right and a left tieback. Lay the batting on a flat surface to avoid confusion. Fold the tieback batting in half to determine the appropriate position for the star block. Lay the block approximately 1" in from the center fold of the tieback. Pin the star block to the batting with the right side facing up. Cut a 1½" × 12" strip from the tieback background print. Lay the long side of the strip over the raw edge of the star block along the upper and lower block edges. Sew the side with a ¼" seam through all the layers. Open the strip, and press it flat with an iron. Trim the strip to the contour shape of the batting. With the balance of the tieback background fabric, lay a straight side to one of the block sides and pin

the raw edges together. Sew a ¼" seam through all the layers. Open and press flat. Turn to the batting side of the tieback and trim the background fabric to the shape of the batting. Repeat this process for the remaining side of the star block. Press.

3. Referring to Making Piping in the Glossary, construct piping from one of the prints used in the block. Sew the piping around the curved edge of the tieback, clipping into the piping seam allowance to flatten the trim.

4. Cut the lining from the tieback pattern. With right sides facing each other, sew the layers together in the seam used to attach the piping. Leave a 6" opening along the lower back side of the tieback. Clip into the curves up to the seam allowance before reversing. Reverse and machine- or hand-stitch the opening closed.

5. Use hook-and-loop tape to secure the tieback ends together and to fasten the tieback to the curtain and/or the molding.

PART THREE

PATCHWORK AROUND THE HOUSE

Since quilting entered my life, many things have changed. I am never bored, I prefer shopping for fabric to any other purchase, and I save the smallest strip of fabric for future and as yet unknown projects. Visualizing patchwork motifs throughout the rooms of the house, in addition to on the bed, provides new outlets for creative energies. Fabric odds and ends can be used with great success for this purpose. Cotton calico works best for the projects in this section, as it will launder well and minimize fading.

The overlock or serger is the ideal tool for tablecloths, shower curtains, and napkins. With a rolled hem, a finished edge or a constructional seam is completed attractively in little or no time. Since the popularity of sergers has increased, great numbers of home sewers do their own sergers. Hopefully the projects featured in this book will inspire you to find new serger applications, so you'll rarely put the machine's cover over its head. I'm certain you will put the serger back in its box only when company comes to visit.

For the conventional sewing machine there are applications for some of the exciting built-in decorative stitches. I know that many of you bought the model that had sixty-six stitches over the machine model that only had thirty-four because you felt it was the last machine you would ever buy and sought the most for your money. Unfortunately, most sewers use their upgraded models the same as they did their old straight-stitch sewing machines. There are exciting threads and products available to make you an instant success with machine embroidery. You need not reserve these applications to construction of clothing for small children. Embroider a cotton strip and put it on a guest towel, tablecloth, napkin edge, or lampshade. Once you have fused an appliqué to a background, use one of those decorative stitches to secure the raw edges. As you become more accustomed to the stitch formations you will see endless opportunities for their use.

Visit household departments and bed and bath shops for new ideas. Fingertip towels trimmed with a bit of lace or an appliqué are very costly. But you can purchase an irregular towel and, using a band of decoratively trimmed fabric and lace, convert a modest purchase into a lovely gift.

PLATE 4. Sewing Room Window Treatment

PLATE 5. Broderie Perse Curtains

PLATE 6. Delph House Appliqué Curtains and Country Heart Valance

PLATE 7. Pieced Tulip Curtain

PLATE 1. Country Patchwork Curtains

PLATE 2. Sawtooth–Bordered Curtains

PLATE 3. Vertical Stripped Curtains and Jumbo Pleated Valance

PLATE 8. Bargello Valance

PLATE 9. Country Rose Valance and Tiebacks

PLATE 10. Ribboned Tulip Valance and Tulip Bud Tiebacks

PLATE 11. Spiral Patchwork Tiebacks

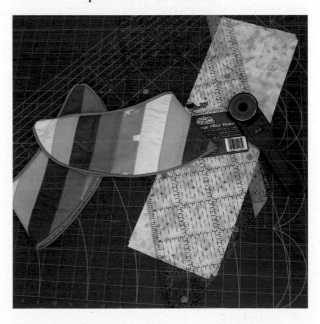

PLATE 12. Sweet Stars Valance and Sweet Star Tiebacks

PLATE 13. Grandmother's Fan Valance and Fan Tiebacks

PLATE 14. Bleeding Heart Table Runner

PLATE 15. Sunflowers for the Kitchen Plate Holder and Centerpiece

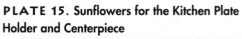
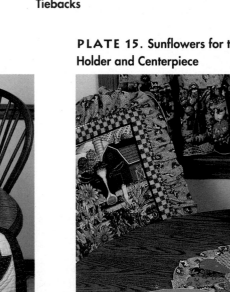

PLATE 17. Tissue Box Cover

PLATE 16. Appliqué Shower Curtain

PLATE 18. Teatime Tablecloth and Accessories

PLATE 19. Battenburg Patchwork Pillow Sham

PLATE 20. Old Linen and Lace Pillow Sham

PLATE 21. Patchwork Dust Ruffle

PLATE 22. Boston Commons Tablecloth

PLATE 23. Sewing Tool Caddy and Box

PLATE 24.
Appliance Covers

PLATE 25. Holiday Place Mats

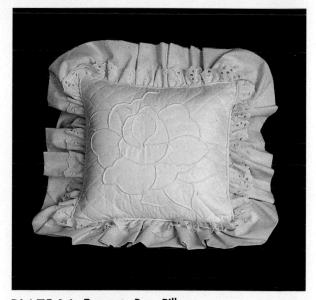

PLATE 26. Trapunto Rose Pillow

PLATE 27. Southwest Pleated Window Shade

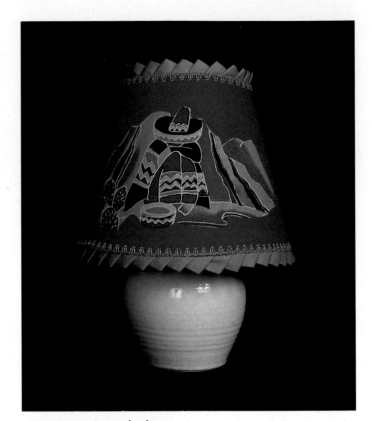

PLATE 28. Lampshade

PLATE 29. Rosette Balloon Window Shades

PLATE 30. A Bear's Fairy-Tale Window Shade

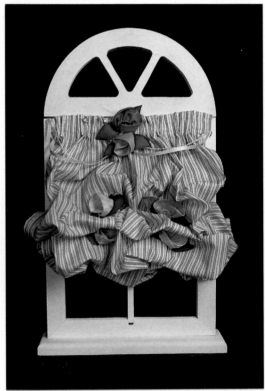

15
TEATIME ACCESSORIES

Fabric manufactures tempt us with wonderful fabric lines. Starting with a large-motif fabric, frequently referred to as a "cheater cloth," they present several coordinating prints and solids to complete the designer look. While the patterns come and go, we will continue to see fabric presented to consumers in this format. It offers convenience and guaranteed success in coordinating colors and prints. The projects in the photograph illustrate such a line. While the tablecloth instructions follow in detail, reviewing the fast methods to complete the additional accessories may prove helpful.

The towels used in these projects were purchased at a local outlet. The cow border was cut and fused with Wonder-Under™ to the border strip of each towel. To prevent the raw edge from lifting with frequent laundering, I used a sewing machine feather-stitch in an accent thread color. The firmness of the towel fabric made it unnecessary to stablize the backing. If you add an embellishment to the looped area of terrycloth, position a wash-away stablizer over the fabric on the right side. This will keep the loops of the cloth from interfering with the feed dog or presser foot of the sewing machine. The towel with the teapot appliqué uses a piping application. I cut a wide band from a striped fabric, thus giving the appearance of strip piecing. Sew piping to the outer edges. Turn the piping over to the wrong side, and straight-stitch in the ditch of the piping attachment seam, going through to the towel to secure the band in place. Attach a larger motif cutout to the center of the towel with Wonder-Under. Trim the outside raw edge with a decorative stitch.

The blue place mat was purchased sometime before the construction of these accessories. I cut out one large motif frequently used for a pillow front within the fabric line, and fused it on point to the place mat rectangular shape. Decorative quilting anchored this square.

The final accessory is the tea cozy. Use discarded fabric to test a suitable shape to cover a favorite teapot. You may consider tracing a shape from an old cozy. Use a solid or light-color print and fuse a large motif to the center of the cozy shape.

Fusing batting to the wrong side of the cozy will provide the stabilizer required for decorative stitching as well as the insulation to maintain the heat of the hot beverage. Draw lines around the appliqué to use as a guide and embellish again with those wonderful decorative stitches. If your sewing machine has only a few simple stitches to choose from, experiment with stitch length and width settings using metallic and decorative threads to achieve variety. Lace trim was used on the edge as well as piping to give a clean outline. Lining the cozy makes for a simpler and neater finish. Sew the top edges of the outer cozy together. Cut the lining the same size as the outside shell, seam the top edge, and lay the front and lining together, with right sides facing. Sew along the lower edge, leaving an opening for reversing. Clip into curves, reverse, and topstitch the opening closed. It is always preferable to leave the opening in the lining.

TEATIME TABLECLOTH

Use paper to make a pattern from your tabletop. While this may seem awkward, keep in mind that you need trace only one quarter of the table to create the pattern. The two inside straight edges of the paper will each be placed on the fold of your fabric or cut from four strip segments and assembled into one unit. The design can be redrawn for each quarter of the circle, or you may reproduce the motif for each of the four sections of the tablecloth. Lay the paper on the table surface and trace the tabletop edge with a pencil for an accurate pattern. You may reproduce the four paper sections and tape them together to check the size and yardage requirements.

MATERIALS

(Based on a 40″ round tabletop)
1 yard of each of five coordinating prints

¼ yard of cotton lace
6½ yards of piping made from one of the five

prints used in the strip-piecing construction

6½ yards of 2½″ bias ruffling made from one of the five prints used in the strip-piecing construc-tion. The yardage provided above for the prints includes the amount required to make the ruffle.

Matching Woolly Nylon™ thread

INSTRUCTIONS

1. Using a rotary cutter, cut strips at least 2″ wide from all the fabrics. Cut the strips lengthwise when using striped fabric. Cut the lace crosswise.

2. With Woolly Nylon thread in the upper looper, piece the strips together with a rolled hem, wrong sides together. Use the paper pattern as a guide to determine the dimension you will require, then cut out the four quarters of the tablecloth.

3. With wrong sides together, roll-hem the table-cloth quarters together.

4. Refer to Making Piping in the Glossary. Sew the piping to the outside raw edge of the cloth.

The piping reinforces the edge, and stabilizes the fabric against stretching and distorting the shape.

5. Construct 2½″ bias strips and use a rolled hem with the Woolly Nylon to finish the outer edge. Refer to the Glossary for New Options for Gathering Ruffles.

6. Overlock the ruffle to the piping seam on the wrong side to complete the cloth. Bias ruffling is used on the edge of a rounded shape because the grainline maintains the upright shape of the ruffle.

16
BLEEDING HEART TABLE RUNNER

This charming runner was designed and executed by a dear quilting friend and teacher, Bobbie Brannin. She prefers hand piecing and hand quilting, and this charming cloth is a product of her accomplished talents. If you maintain a short (1.5 mm to 2 mm) stitch length on your sewing machine, this project can be successfully pieced on your machine. The runner features four paired blocks of the design with a quilted wreath in the center position. The block size is 14½" and the completed runner measures 16½" x 74".

MATERIALS

¾ yard of 100% cotton background print

½ yard of 100% cotton red print

1 yard of 100% cotton dark green border print

2 yards of lining

2 yards of polyester batting

Matching sewing and quilting threads

Plastic template material

INSTRUCTIONS

1. Prewash and iron the fabrics for this project.

2. Trace the patterns onto plastic template material and refer to the block diagram provided on the next page for a cutting guide.

3. Mark the fabrics on the wrong side and cut the appropriate shapes from each fabric.

4. Refer to the block diagram and piece the light background A units to either side of the red B unit. Piece with a small running stitch. Sew the light background corner C square to the top of B. Repeat the process for the remaining three corner sections.

5. Assemble the center section, stitching the E units to the four curved sides of the F unit. Attach a D unit to each of the four straight sides of the center section. Trimming the seam allowance in the curved areas to ⅛″ will minimize the need to clip into the concave seams. Press. Complete the block assembly by sewing the corner sections to the center motif. Press. Repeat steps 3 through 5 for each of the remaining three blocks.

6. Sew two of the four blocks together to form a block pair. Repeat for the remaining two blocks to form a second pair.

7. Sew each of the two block pairs to either side of a 14½″ plain block, which you cut from the light background fabric.

8. In the center mark the quilting motif provided below. The blocks are quilted ¼″ from the seam allowance, and at ½″ intervals in the outer background curves.

9. Cut two 2″-wide border strips lengthwise on the grain of the fabric and sew these to the long sides of the runner. Cut two more 2″-wide border strips for the short sides of the runner. Attach the border strips with a ¼″ seam allowance. Press.

10. Baste the top, batting, and lining together, working from the center out to the sides. Quilt the runner.

11. Fold ¼″ of the raw edge of the border and bring it over to the wrong side of the runner. Blindstitch the border to the wrong side of the cloth with matching thread.

BLEEDING HEART TABLE RUNNER QUILTING MOTIF

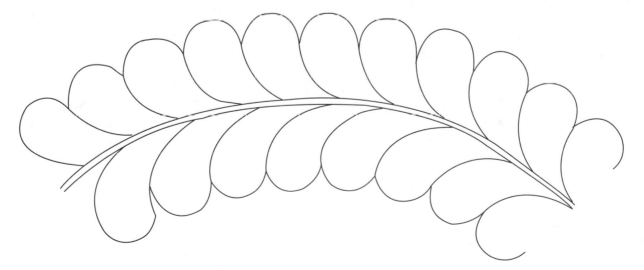

BLEEDING HEART TABLE RUNNER
PATTERN AND DIAGRAM

Add ¼" seam allowance.
Enlarge to size indicated in piecing diagram.

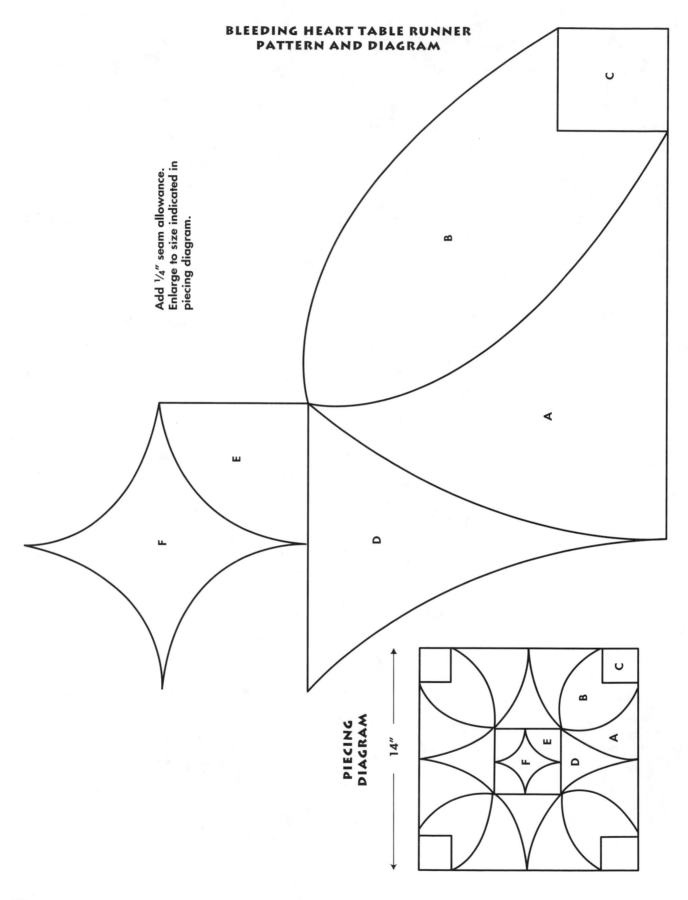

PIECING DIAGRAM

14"

17
SUNFLOWERS FOR THE KITCHEN

The grouping of sunflower accessories in the photograph features a preprinted panel and assorted coordinated prints within a fabric line. I added a small variety of additional gold prints and selected a single element of the panel design, the sunflowers, to use with some accessories. The panels are certainly appealing, and using them for chair backs shows them off to advantage.

Use fusible batting and a minimal amount of quilting to make chair backs in little time. The ruffle was cut on the bias to ensure that it would stand away from the chair and not fall limp upon itself. The cushion ties are made of two layers of fabric, fused together with Wonder-Under™. The edge of the ties was finished with a rolled hem using Woolly Nylon™ on the serger. General construction techniques for the lampshade are provided on pages 89–90. The farm animals are cutouts from the coordinating fabric fused to the background using Wonder-Under. A bit of machine embroidery in variegated green thread was added to the lampshade for texture.

SUNFLOWER PLATE HOLDER

MATERIALS

⅛ yard of each of five gold or yellow prints for the sunflower petals

4″ square for sunflower center

½ yard of background fabric for the front and back

1 yard of muslin for the inner circles

1¼ yards of iron-on heavy-weight nonwoven interfacing

Complementary Woolly Nylon™ thread

Matching sewing threads

Plastic template material

Freezer paper

INSTRUCTIONS

1. Determine the size of the plates you will be using in the storage cover. Add 2″ to the plate diameter to figure the required circle size. Make a pattern of the circle you will need. Cut two circles from paper and test them with a plate to make certain the circle is large enough to cover the plates.

2. Draw the petal pattern onto the plastic template material. Mark fifteen segments using the template, three on each of the five prints. Cut out the petals and arrange them on a flat surface to select the final order. Sew the petals together using a ¼″ seam allowance. Turn the outside edge under a scant ¼″, baste, and press. Using the small circle pattern provided, cut one small circle from freezer paper. Iron the circle of paper to the wrong side of the flower center fabric with the coated side pressed to the wrong side of the fabric. Cut out the fabric circle, adding a ¼″ seam allowance as you cut. Baste the seam allowance over the paper pattern. Keep the thread knot on the surface of the work.

3. Using a decorative stitch on your sewing machine, sew the circle to the center of the flower. Remove the basting stitches, and carefully peel away the paper pattern from the flower back.

4. Cut two plate-size circles from the outer fabric and two from iron-on interfacing. Fuse the interfacing to the wrong side of the fabric circles. Using the same decorative stich apply the sunflower to one circle for the storage top.

5. For the inside layers, cut six plate-size circles from lining fabric and six of iron-on interfacing. Fuse the interfacing to the fabric wrong side of the lining circles.

6. Finish the raw edges of the circles using a rolled hem stitch with Woolly Nylon in the upper looper.

7. With matching thread or nylon monofilament thread start to sew the circles together along half their circumference. Position the top outer circle with the sunflower with a lining circle underneath. Keep the outer edges aligned. Sew the two together close to the edge and going through only half of the circumference of the circles. Lay the second lining circle under the previous lining circle and stitch the two together along half their outer edge on the side opposite the sewn edge of the first outer fabric and lining circles. Continue joining the remaining circles, alternating the side of the stitching path as each layer is added. Add the second outer fabric circle (the bottom) last with right side showing out. With alternating openings you can insert plates between the layers for an attractive and practical method of storage.

SUNFLOWER PLATE HOLDER PATTERN

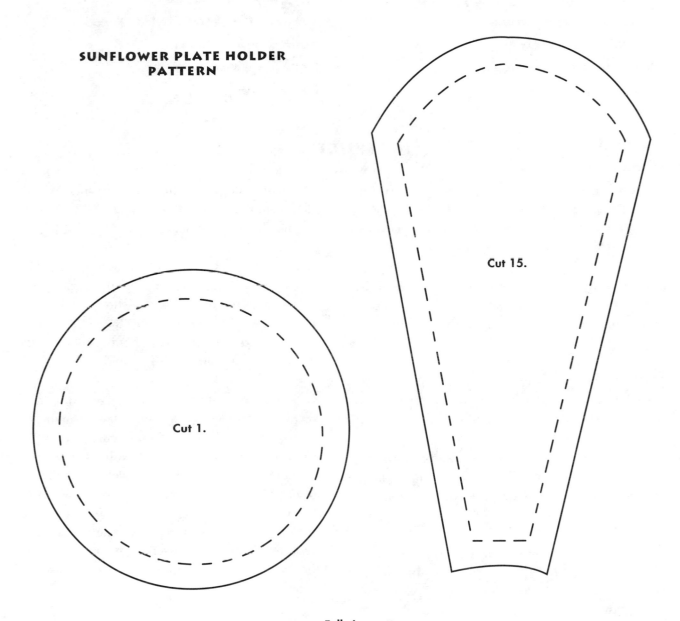

Cut 1.

Cut 15.

Full-size pattern

SUNFLOWER CENTERPIECE

MATERIALS

⅛ yard of each of five gold or yellow prints

⅓ yard of background print

⅓ yard of polyester batting

4″ square for sunflower center

½ yard of print for ruffle

Tear-away fabric stabilizer

Complementary Woolly Nylon™ thread

Matching sewing threads

Plastic template material

Freezer paper

INSTRUCTIONS

1. Trace the pattern for the petals, provided for step 2 of the Sunflower Plate Holder project, page 60, onto plastic template material. Cut six pieces from each of the five gold prints.

2. Using a ¼″ seam allowance, piece one complete flower together using fifteen segments. Piece the remaining sections into two half flowers.

3. Follow steps 2 and 3 of the Sunflower Plate Holder directions, page 60, to prepare the small circle for the center of the sunflower.

4. Lay the complete flower on the background fabric. Add the two half flowers to either side, referring to the photograph of the centerpiece for positioning guidance.

5. Using a tear-away stabilizer such as Stitch-N-Tear™, Tearaways™, or typing-weight paper behind the wrong side of the front, appliqué the flower piece to the background fabric with a decorative stitch. After the appliqué is secure, pull away the stabilizer.

6. Use the flower appliqué as a guide for trimming the background material: Mark ½″ beyond the outside edges of the appliqué and cut the background fabric on the marked line. Cut a batting and a lining the same size.

7. Refer to New Options for Gathering Ruffles in the Glossary and prepare a bias strip for the ruffle that is twice the length of the outside edge and 2″ wide. The raw edge on the ruffle shown was finished with a rolled hem using Woolly Nylon thread in the upper looper.

8. Sew the ruffle to the outside edge of the mat, keeping the raw edges in line. Sew through the front layer and the batting. Secure the ruffle safely out of the stitching path with safety pins or masking tape. Lay the front over the backing, and sew the layers together following the seamline made when attaching the ruffle. Leave an opening of about 6″ along one straight side. Clip into the curves before reversing the project. Fold the seam allowance in on the opening and stitch by machine or hand to close.

9. Machine-quilt through all the layers around the center circle and in several of the petal seams. This minimal quilting will hold the project together adequately for normal use.

18
APPLIANCE COVERS

To spruce up any kitchen at little cost, stitch covers for the appliances you use most and keep on the countertop. If you like, employ a motif or construction technique that coordinates with your curtains. This offers another opportunity to utilize the decorative stitchery of your sewing machine.

Appliance sizes vary from manufacturer to manufacturer and from one year to the next. Measure the height, width, and depth of the appliance. Add ½″ for a seam allowance to the measurements. Before cutting the fabric for the final project, make a mock-up from an old sheet or scrap cloth. Baste the seams together without finishing the raw edges. Try the sample on the appliance and evaluate the fit. Is it too tight? Can you comfortably bring the cover over the handles as well as over the appliance itself? If the cover shrinks, will it still fit? Often an additional ½″ in width or depth will make the difference between a too-snug cover and one that fits like the commercially made product. Add that ½″ onto another sample panel, cut, baste, and try the new cover on. Only when you are satisfied with the end result is it time to cut the cover out of the "real fabric" you planned for the project. You will require an amount of lining and batting equal to whatever yardage you need for the outside cover. If you use a prequilted fabric for part of the cover, you can eliminate the required batting in this area. Select a cotton-weight fabric and "beef it up" with iron-on interfacing. Appliqué the cover before assembling the parts. Referring to Making Piping in the Glossary, add piping to the seams. This adds a crisp and professional finish to the cover. Finally, it is always preferable to line the cover, leaving the opening in a lining seam, than to bind the hem edges. The lining provides additional body to the cover, permitting it to stand on its own.

The following are common sizes and corresponding yardages for some of the most popular appliance covers:

Two-Slice toaster cover: 9¼″ high × 15″ wide ×

9¼″ deep—½ yard of each of the outer fabric lining, and batting.

Coffeemaker cover: 10½″ high × 11½″ wide × 10¼″ deep—½ yard of each of the outer fabric and lining.

Crock-Pot™ cover: 14″ diameter (across) top × 9″ high × 39½″ circumference—½ yard of each of the outer fabric, lining, and batting.

These yardages demonstrate that the fabric requirements and cost will be minimal.

The following directions illustrate the basic method of construction used to make all the covers.

COFFEEMAKER COVER

MATERIALS

½ yard of background fabric for front and back panels

½ yard of accent print for sides/top panel

1 yard of iron-on interfacing

Assorted scraps of cotton prints for appliqués

Wonder-Under™ for fusing appliqués to panels

Piping, either purchased or made from matching fabric

Tear-away fabric stabilizer

Matching sewing threads

INSTRUCTIONS

1. Derive a correctly sized pattern for the appliance following the suggestions given above. Cut the front and back panels, and the sides/top panel from outer fabric and lining material.

2. Fuse interfacing to any fabric sections that are not prequilted.

3. Use Wonder-Under according to manufacturer's directions to fuse appliqués to the back and front. Stabilize the wrong side of the panels with a tear-away product (such as Stitch-N-Tear™ or typing-weight paper to ensure a good quality stitch. Loosen the needle tension on your sewing machine for correct formation of the decorative stitching. Use a satin stitch, buttonhole stitch, or featherstitch to secure the raw edges of the appliqués to the background. The covers photographed use the same motifs provided on page 14 for the Delph House Appliqué Curtains. Embellish the interior of the small houses with machine stitchery.

4. Align the raw edges of the piping with the cover panels and stitch the piping in place. Join the front and back together, stitch the sides/top panel to the piping seams.

5. Use a $\frac{1}{4}''$ seam allowance and sew the lining sections together, leaving a 7″ opening along one seam. The opening should be within the seam and not at the seam edge. Sew piping to the lower outside edge of the cover. Position the lining over the cover with right sides facing each other. Pin in place. Stitch the two together in the lower piping seamline.

6. Turn the cover right side out, and machine-stitch the opening closed to complete.

19
PATCHWORK DUST RUFFLE

Dust ruffles can be quickly made to complement one or several quilts. By making your own dust ruffle, you can also construct it so that changing the bed is easy. Often dust ruffles are made by attaching a scantily gathered length of fabric (within a limited palette of colors) to a nylon tricot sheet designed to be positioned between mattress and box spring. Installing the tricot layer smoothly between the bedding becomes quite a difficult chore. How much easier to use an old cotton/polyester sheet cut to the bed size. With the use of shirring tapes (available in either sew-in or iron-on installations), the ruffle can be gathered evenly and sewn to the sheet within a few hours.

MATERIALS

In order to determine the yardage required for the project, measure the drop of the bed from the edge of the box spring to the floor. A common figure for this is 15", but, it may vary by several inches. Combine the side lengths of the bed and add the bed width. A twin bed has a length of 75" and a width of 39"; the overall length of the three sides is 75" times 2 plus 39", which equals 189". The dust ruffle photographed features a flying geese design. I choose to double the length of the three sides to determine the overall fullness of the dust ruffle. The fullness may vary from 2 to

$2\frac{1}{2}$ times the perimeter of the three sides of the mattress. Too much fullness may hide an added detail such as an appliqué along the edge or within the skirt. Twice the length will provide sufficient fullness and still be more generous than a store-bought dust ruffle.

The drop was measured at 15". With an insert of 3", the skirt pictured required a finished 12" width of background fabric. Adding $\frac{1}{2}$" for a seam allowance because of serger construction, I required a $12\frac{1}{2}$" length of fabric in sufficient crosswise cuts to yield a total yardage of twice the bed perimeter. I multiplied 189" times 2, yielding 378", and divided this amount by the width of the fabric I was using, or 44". The

amount according to my calculator was 8.59. Rounding off the math, I cut nine $12\frac{1}{2}$" sections for the basic skirt. Nine times $12\frac{1}{2}$" is $112\frac{1}{2}$" or 3.13 yards. I would need a 3.13-yard length of patchwork as well for the dust ruffle border. The sample photographed shows the wonderful flying geese border, and this was quickly obtained from a striped fabric that had a repeat of this design appearing three times on each length of the cloth. I purchased $1\frac{1}{4}$ yards of this border fabric, and cut $\frac{1}{4}$" beyond the flying geese print using the rotary cutter.

The amount of shirring tape needed will be the same length as the fabric used to construct the dust ruffle, 3.13 yards for the skirt shown.

INSTRUCTIONS

1. With a rolled hem setting on the serger, attach, as I did, the border band to the $12\frac{1}{2}$" background section to form the dust ruffle. You can quickly attach the border band the way I did. I used a rolled hem piecing method, using Woolly Nylon™ thread in the upper looper.

2. Finish the long outside edges of the ruffle with a rolled hem on the serger as well.

3. Iron $\frac{1}{2}$" of the top edge of the dust ruffle down, and fuse or sew the shirring tape to it. Tie the cord ends into a secure knot, and position the tape $\frac{1}{2}$" from the top edge. Pin into position carefully to minimize shifting. Sew or fuse the

tape to the fabric following the tape manufacturer's specific directions.

4. Tie the cord ends together, and draw up the cord to gather the ruffle.

5. Match the ruffle corner to the sheet corner, and pin in place. Topstitch the ruffle to the sheet, sewing across one short end of the tape to prevent it from drawing up as you work. I prefer leaving the cord ends tucked into the wrong side of the dust ruffle. Loosening the pleats will permit the completed ruffle to dry quickly when laundered.

20
APPLIQUÉ SHOWER CURTAIN SET

With the availablity of shower curtain liners, we are free at last to turn our imagination to the bathroom shower curtain—and matching accessories—as well as the bedroom.

I frequently get great ideas when I go to expensive bath shows. During one such visit I saw costly shower rings that had been covered with fabric.

MATERIALS

A standard curtain for a bath tub shower is 72" × 72". My fabric was 44" wide, and for convenience I doubled this width by seaming two lengths together. The resulting yardage for the project is 4 yards. In addition to this fabric you will need ½ yard for a top facing and the same amount of Wonder-Under™. I also used ½ yard of each of two coordinating solids for bias trims.

INSTRUCTIONS

1. Begin with the shower ring covers. Use a 9½" length of bias strip cut 2" wide and sew the long sides together. Reverse the tube (for one turn-ing technique, see Using a Fasturn™ in the Glossary). Press.

2. Finish one end and slide the tubes over the plastic shower curtain rings.

3. Trace a curve provided in Part Two for valance edges or use one outlined on your rotary cutter mat. (The curve you require should be approximately 8″ in length. If the available curve is 6″, simply lengthen the pattern by inserting a 2″ section in the middle of the curve). Begin 1″ in from the curtain side, and mark the top edge on the wrong side.

4. Cut ¼″ away from the top edge marked line for a seam allowance.

5. Cut bias strips 1½″ in width from the coordinating solid fabric.

6. With the aid of the Fasturn, reverse the tubes, then press them with the seam in the back.

7. Start with one color tube, and pin to form a curve from the middle of one top scalloped edge, skipping the next scallop, and completing the shape in the middle of the next curve. Repeat this procedure with the second color, until the colored tubes intersect each other.

8. Stitch the tube bands in place after checking that they are positioned an equal distance from the top edge. The strips in the shower curtain photographed were stitched in place using an outline scallop stitch. The raw edges of the bands can be cut and extended into the seam allowance of the top raw edge.

9. Cut twelve 3″ × 2″ rectangles of facing fabric and twelve Wonder-Under rectangles of the same size. Fuse the Wonder-Under to the wrong side of the facing fabric. On the wrong side of the rectangles, centered within the cut sections, draw a small rectangle with your marker 1¾″ × ½″.

10. Position the marked rectangles with their right sides to the right side of the curtain, 1″ down from the scallop point. Sew on the lines of the marked rectangle.

11. Cut through all the layers, down the center of the inner rectangle and cutting into the angles at the four corners.

12. Reverse the rectangle piece to the wrong side of the curtain front, remove the paper from the wrong side of the Wonder-Under backing, and press to fuse the rectangle in place. This will create a clean finished opening.

13. The top edge of the curtain will be faced to complete the ribbon openings. Cut two widths 6″ long from a lining fabric and seam these together along the short side.

14. Hem the lower edge of the facing with a rolled hem using the serger, or hem on the sewing machine.

15. Position the curtain front to the right side of the facing, and stitch the top edges together. Clip into the curves, reverse, and iron.

16. Transfer placement markings to the facing of the ribbon openings by tracing along the cutout areas on the front. Cut Wonder-Under rectangles 3″ × 2″ and repeat the same method used on the curtain front to make the ribbon openings.

17. Complete the sides and lower edges of the curtain with a serged rolled hem.

18. To make the ribbons that attach the curtain to the rings, use two layers of fabric and cut them 1½″ in width. Fuse them together with Wonder-Under. Finish with a rolled serged hem using Woolly Nylon™ in the upper looper.

APPLIQUÉ TISSUE BOX COVER

MATERIALS

½ yard of box fabric

½ yard of lining fabric

½ yard of polyester batting

¼ yard of accent fabric for fabric rose

¼ yard hook-and-loop tape

Matching sewing threads

INSTRUCTIONS

1. Using your tissue box as the guide to create the pattern, wrap the box fabric around the shape as you would when wrapping a gift. The opening in the box lid will serve as the opening for the cover, so bring the fabric ends to meet at the opening edges.

At each side of the opening you will need to seam the fabrics together. Stitch the raw edges within the opening area flat without joining their abutting edges.

2. The sides of the box cover should be folded into triangular overlapping flaps, as you fold when wrapping a gift. Trim away excess fabric, until the flaps of the sides overlap approximately ½″. One side may be permanently stitched in

place. The remaining side will serve as the opening to insert the tissue box. Secure this opening with hook-and-loop tape.

3. Using the pattern provided for the rosettes featured in the Rosette Balloon Window Shade, page 94, cut a rosette from the accent fabric.

4. Trim the straight edge of the rosette with string pearls, referring to Attaching Beads with a Serger in the Glossary.

5. Gather the rosette along the curved side into a bud shape.

6. Stitch the rosette to the side of the opening of the tissue box.

21
OLD LINEN AND LACE PILLOW SHAM

Many sewers have a collection of linens, doilies, or odds and ends of antique lace. It seems a pity to disgard the workmanship and care put into the creation of these items. Combining your handwork with the treasures of an earlier family member is the perfect marriage of design and function. Pillow shams offer an appropriate format to display antique needlework. The shams are ornamental for the most part, with little hard use. Several seasons, indeed years, can pass before the necessity of laundering the sham. Anticipate the hardships of cleaning, and secure the needlework with easy-to-remove basting stitches.

The sham pictured in the photograph uses an old antimacassar as an accent. For the sham, I selected a white and beige neutral fabric whose large printed roses had an antique feeling. I cut this background fabric to the size I required, adding a seam allowance. Take the linen or lace with you to select fabric. Lay the antique piece on the bolt to preview the overall effect before purchasing. The white and tan coloration of the background prevented the antimacassar from appearing too discolored. Covering the lower corners of the linen with Grandmother's Fan seemed an appropriate pattern choice. This quilt motif is frequently embellished with buttons and laces that are a perfect complement to an old linen.

MATERIALS

¾ yard of background fabric for pillow front

¾ yard of backing fabric

¾ yard of lining muslin

¾ yard of polyester batting

1 yard of ruffle fabric

5 yards of lace trim

⅛ yard of each of six prints for the fan segments

Buttons, ribbons, beads for embellishing the fan segments

Matching sewing threads

INSTRUCTIONS

1. Measure the bed pillow to be covered. A standard pillow will take a front cover of 24″ × 18″. Naturally, queen- and king-size pillows are different dimensions, and the pillow filling will alter the thickness, so use a tape measure to determine the size needed. Add at least a ½″ seam allowance to all sides.

2. Position the batting and the lining behind the wrong side of the pillow front and pin or thread-baste the layers together. Machine- or hand-quilt the top. I quilted around the large floral motifs; however, you may fill in the background using a large grid pattern. Refer to Marking a Gridded Quilting Pattern in the Glossary for specific instructions.

3. Use the fan pattern on page 45 and make two complete fan units.

4. Arrange the antique needlework over the pillow front, adding fan segments to the center, or to either side of the linen as illustrated by the photograph. Sew through the layers to anchor the linen to the background. The buttons and embroidery were attached with a sewing machine. This all can be removed at a later time to salvage the old linens when the pillow sham looks too worn for further use.

5. Cut the ruffle fabric into 8″ bias strips. Sew the strips together and gather the layers according to the suggestions provided in New Options for Gathering Ruffles in the Glossary. Stitch the lace to the pillow raw edge first, then attach the ruffle.

6. Hold down the ruffle securely to the front with masking tape to keep it out of the seamline.

7. Cut two 18 ½″ × 16″ sections for the backing. The size of the back sections should be the pillow height by half the width plus 4″ for overlapping. Hem one short side of each back section. Overlap the two until they are the same size as the pillow front. Stitch the overlap area together within the ¼″ outside seam allowance.

8. With right sides facing each other, lay the pillow front over the pillow back sections, and pin the layers together carefully. Stitch the back and the front together in the stitching line previously used to attach the ruffle. Sew around the entire outer edge. Reverse the pillow sham through the back opening after trimming the excess fabric from the seam allowance on all four corners. Remove the masking tape that held the ruffle out of harm's way during the final construction.

22
BATTENBERG PATCHWORK PILLOW SHAM

I have long been an admirer of Battenberg lace needlework. In traditional Battenberg, the empty areas created within the outline designs of tape are filled with a variety of hand embroidery stitches. Like most quilters, I never discard a usable piece of fabric or a section of patchwork remaining from a previous project. In this project, once my taped design was established, I took a section of strip piecing and laid it behind the empty center section of the basket pattern.

Designing patterns for this Battenberg method is as simple as tracing a shape if you use quilters' double pencils, which are joined at the points with small rubber wedges. These pencils, available at most quilt shops, are commonly used for tracing a template and marking the $\frac{1}{4}''$ quilting lines. Trace a design with the double pencils, and the lines will provide the position for Battenberg tape placement.

MATERIALS

¾ yard of background fabric for the pillow front

¾ yard of backing fabric for pillow

¾ yard of muslin for lining

¾ yard of polyester batting

1 yard of fabric for ruffle

5 yards of Battenberg tape with or without picot edge

Water-soluble fabric stabilizer

Button trims

INSTRUCTIONS

1. Cut out the pillow front referring to step 1 of the pillow sham instructions on page 72 for guidelines in cutting the proper dimensions. Referring to Gridding Lines and Right-Angle Triangles in the Glossary, mark a $1\frac{1}{2}''$ grid on the pillow front. Machine-quilt the front in matching thread.

2. Trace the design for the basket onto water-soluble fabric stabilizer such as Solvy™. Lay the tape over the lines and pull the tape string gently to manipulate the edges around the curves. Pin the tape securely to the stabilizer to hold the design in place. Tuck the tape ends under the work. Use white thread and a narrow zigzag to stitch the tape to the stabilizer.

3. Cut a small assortment of $1\frac{1}{2}''$ strips to create the patchwork filler for the basket. Lay the first strip with the right side up and attach an additional strip to one raw edge with a $\frac{1}{4}''$ seam. Press the strips open and flat. Add additional strips using the same method until the unit is large enough to fill the center of the basket. Sew the tape to the patchwork. Pull away the water soluble stabilizer in front of the patchwork.

4. The leaves and butterflies are cut from large floral prints and appliquéd to the background with a satin stitch.

5. Attach the lace basket to the background with a small zigzag or straight stitch. The flowers are formed by creating four tape loops and tacking them down in the center. Stitch a button in the center of each flower.

6. Prepare an 8″ bias strip for ruffling. Gather the ruffle, referring to New Options for Gathering Ruffles in the Glossary for specific directions. Attach the ruffle to the pillow front. Follow steps 6 and 7 of the pillow sham instructions on page 72 to complete the pillow backing.

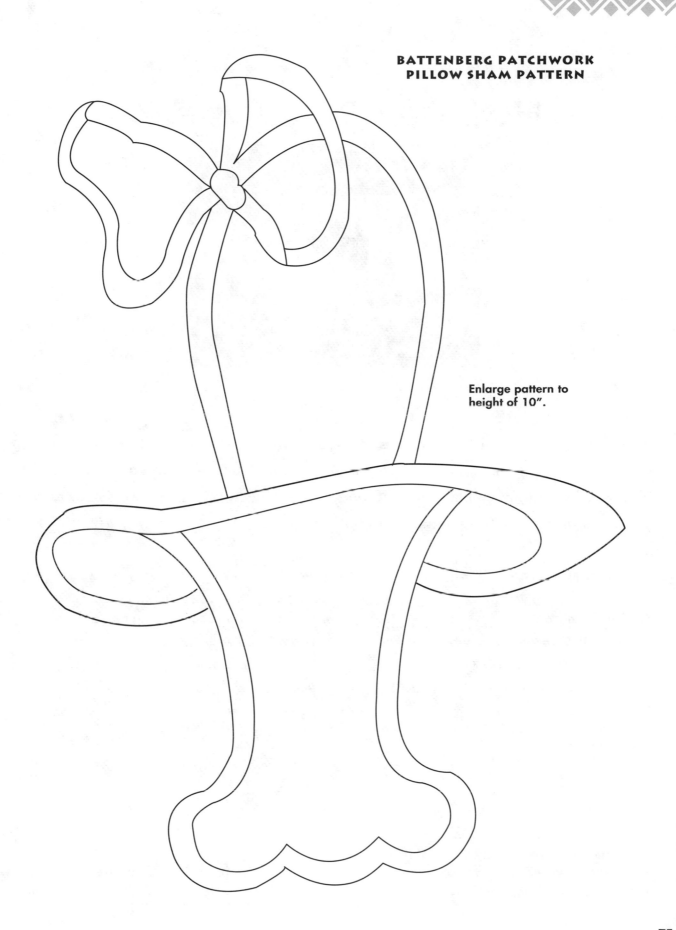

Enlarge pattern to
height of 10″.

23
HOLIDAY PLACE MATS

These place mats are quick to make and require little or no hand stitching. The batting of choice for this project is a fusible fleece. When completed and pressed, these will look as finished as purchased place mats. If you substitute the holiday fabric with an attractive print, this design will be delightful for everyday use.

MATERIALS

(For four place mats)

1 yard of 100% cotton background fabric

¼ yard of 100% cotton accent fabric

¼ yard of 100% cotton lace with scalloped edging

1 yard of 100% cotton fabric in accent color for piping and bias

1 yard of 100% cotton backing fabric

1 yard of fusible fleece batting

½ yard Wonder-Under™

Tear-away fabric stabilizer

Template material

INSTRUCTIONS

1. Trace the teardrop shape onto plastic template material. Trace four Wonder-Under teardrop shapes for each place mat. Position the shape over the wrong side of the accent fabric and fuse in place. Cut out the fused areas.

2. Cut each place mat front from the background fabric, 13″ × 17″. Position the rounded end of a teardrop toward each corner of the rectangles, and pin these into place. Cut a section from the lace fabric that will be of sufficient size to lay under the middle area between each pair of teardrop appliqués. Cut for a lace underlay, adding at least a ½″ seam allowance. Fuse the teardrops in place, catching the lace edges at the same time.

3. Using a 6″ scallop following the scallop pattern A provided on page 13, mark the middle edges of the place mats to create a curved edge.

4. Cut 1¼″ bias strips for the ribboned band overlapping the appliqué's raw edge. Refer to Using a Fasturn™ in the Glossary. Sew the raw edges of the strips together and reverse. Press the strips, keeping the seam to the back of the strips.

5. Position the strips over the raw edges and use a decorative stitch on the sewing machine to stitch the bands into place. The raw edges of the bands can overlap the place mat edges. For the best stitch formation when attaching the piping trim, stabilize the work. Remove the stabilizer when the stitching is completed.

6. Refer to Making Piping in the Glossary and make at least 13 yards of 1¼″ piping for attaching to the outside edges of the place mats. The piping shown on the photographed place mats was stitched using gold thread and a decorative buttonhole stitch. The simple addition of metallic thread created an expensive-looking piping.

7. Before attaching the piping to the outer edge, fuse the batting to the wrong side of the place mat front. The batting will provide sufficient weight to support the piping. Stitch the piping through all the layers.

8. Position the front over the back and, using the piping stitching line as a guide, sew through all the layers. Leave an opening in the middle of one long side. Clip into the curves up to the seamlines before reversing. Reverse and press. Turn the raw edges on the opening in to the seamline and sew with matching thread to finish the edge. Press the place mat following manufacturer's directions to activate the fusible agent in the batting. Quilt one stitching line within the appliquéd sections, following the curve of the bias to secure the layers.

HOLIDAY PLACE MATS PATTERN

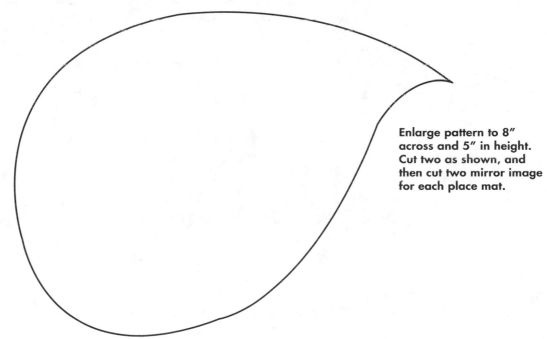

Enlarge pattern to 8″ across and 5″ in height. Cut two as shown, and then cut two mirror image for each place mat.

24
SEWING TOOL CADDY

Organizing the tools of our craft can make life simpler in the sewing room as well as add to its decor. With only a yard of print, make a zippered pouch and cover a box for handy storage.

MATERIALS

1 yard of cotton print

¼ yard of polyester batting

3 zippers 12″ or larger

Matching sewing thread

1 wire coat hanger

INSTRUCTIONS

1. Cut four sections of outer fabric 7″ × 14″. Cut six bands 2″ × 14″ from the outer fabric as well. Baste a pair of the 2″ strips together along their 14″ length, using a ½″ seam allowance, and press the seam flat.

2. Position a closed zipper with its wrong side facing up over the wrong side of the seamed fabric. The zipper tab must be positioned at least ½″ within the seam, and the length can extend beyond the seam if the zipper is larger than the seam length. Baste the zipper in place to prevent it from moving. Using the zipper foot on the sewing machine, work on the right side of the zipper to sew it in place. Use the quilting bar on the sewing machine as a guide, running the flat end of the guide over the seam center to ensure a straight seam. Repeat this procedure until you have all three zippers sewn into the pairs of 2″ bands. If the zippers are longer than 12″, trim their lengths to conform with the band size after stitching them permanently in place.

3. Cut bias strips 1¼″ in width, and refer to Making Piping in the Glossary for construction specifics. Sew piping the length of the first zipper on each side, working on the right side of the fabric. Repeat for the two remaining zippers.

4. With raw edges aligned, position a 7″ × 14″ section over the piping seam and sew in this stitching line. Open and attach another 7″ × 14″ section to the other side of the zipper. This unit will then connect to another new zipper strip, with a 7″ × 14″ piece attached to the other side of that zipper. Continue to connect the zippers and bands together until all three zippers and four sections are joined.

5. Use the wire hanger to outline the shape of the top edge of the sewing caddy. Trim this shape, adding a ½″ seam allowance beyond the hanger line.

6. Cut a lining, batting, and backing the same size as the front. Position the lining right side up,

followed by the batting facing the wrong side of the lining, and then the backing, wrong side facing the batting and right side facing out. Pin this in place, and quilt the layers together.

7. Sew piping to the right side of the lining unit. Lay the caddy front over the right side of the lining and sew the two together in the piping seam around all sides, leaving a small opening at the top where the wire hanger will poke through. Leave one zipper open to reverse the project. Clip into the corners and into any curved seams. Reverse.

8. Starting at the lowest zipper, stitch across the top piping edge of this zipper. Repeat this step for the middle zipper as well. This will create three separate compartments in the caddy. Using wire cutters, cut the hanger until only the top curve that conforms with the caddy edge remains. Wrap batting over the handle top. Insert a bias-turned strip over the batting to finish the hanger top. With the zipper foot, sew close to the lower edge of the hanger to keep the wire in place for hanging.

9. Stitch in the ditch alongside the piping on the sides and lower edge of the caddy to strengthen the construction.

SEWING BOX

This matching little box was covered using a bit of glue, needle, and thread. Trace the sides of the box and cut batting the same size. Glue this to the box. Add at least 1″ overlap to the fabric covering to allow for gluing the raw edges over to the bottom and inside edges. These edges can be concealed with ribbon or felt. A layer of batting was added to the top before the fabric was applied. The needle strawberry was secured to the top fabric with stitching before the fabric was glued into place on the box top. The buttons and embellishments were glued after the fabric was attached to the box top. The trimming added to the top edge was $1\frac{1}{2}$″ of accent fabric finished with a serged rolled hem with Woolly Nylon™ thread in the upper looper. This strip was gathered and positioned in place with fabric glue.

25
TRAPUNTO ROSE PILLOW

Trapunto is an elegant method of adding relief to an outline design by inserting a cording behind the front layer. Many of the fabrics used in home decorating lend themselves wonderfully to this treatment. Large motifs outlined with a raised corded effect or the clean simplicity of design as shown in the photographed sample are appropriate accents for modern, traditional, or country decorating. Cording the outline of a design emphasizes the pattern, making it more visible from a distance. Try this for valances or chair cushions. Until the development of the sewing machine and double needles, this oldest form of quilting was accomplished by double rows of hand stitching. Now with a zigzag sewing machine and a bit of practice you can add this method to your machine-quilting tricks. Experiment with different yarns, colored or neutral, and the various sizes of double needles available. The yarn recommended is readily available through quilting suppliers or at your local card shop. I have had great success with the two-ply gift-wrap yarn sold at neighborhood card stores. White is the easiest to work with as the color does not shadow through the top layer of the fabric. Separate the yarn into one-thread weight. This cord will be inserted through the small hole opening in most sewing machines' throat plate. Draw the yarn through the hole by creating a loop of thread to lead the yarn, or use a wire-loop threader available from a serger supplier. Refer to Machine Trapunto in the Glossary for detailed instructions and illustrations.

MATERIALS

12½" square of tightly woven fabric such as Polished Apple fabric for the pillow front

½ yard of ruffle fabric

12½" square for backing

12½" square of polyester batting

2 yards of 2-ply white gift yarn

2 yards of preruffled 1½" eyelet trim

2 spools of off-white 40-weight embroidery thread

Pillow form

INSTRUCTIONS

1. Trace the rose pattern provided here onto the pillow front fabric using a soft lead pencil or wash-out marking pen.

2. This design can be executed in two manners on your sewing machine. With the aid of a pin-tuck foot and a 12/4.0 double needle you can stitch on the double lines as indicated in the pattern. Or you may find it more convenient to use a darning foot with the 12/4.0 double needle working in a free-motion stitching formation. For free-motion trapunto it will be necessary to drop the feed dogs of your sewing machine, or cover them with a throat plate cover. Refer to your sewing machine manual for free-motion or darning preparation.

3. Secure the marked pillow top in a machine embroidery hoop. Draw the yarn up through the hole in the throat plate. Using the double needle and working in a free-motion operation, stitch on the line drawing of the rose. Begin at the flower center while keeping the hoop stationary, working in a front-to-back sewing path. This operation does not lend itself to sideways stitching. When turning a corner becomes necessary, pivot on the needles, with the right needle making the turn and the left needle repeatedly stitch-

ing in the same hole, until the stitching path has turned 90 degrees, and resume stitching the design with normal sewing. When you end one row of stitching, remember to cut the yarn as well as the threads before you move to a new section of the design.

Additional details, such as leaf veins, can be added within the design when quilting with a single needle.

4. Free the pillow top from the embroidery hoop. Layer batting behind the wrong side of the pillow top. Refer to Marking a Gridded Quilting Pattern in the Glossary. The grid on the photographed pillow is 1" wide. Replace the double needle in your sewing machine with a single 12/80 needle. Baste the layers together with safety pins, and quilt around the flower and within the design where indicated. Quilt on the grid lines.

5. Trim the outside edges even and attach the eyelet trim to the outside edge, stitching a ¼" seam allowance. Prepare a 6½" bias strip for the ruffle that is twice the length of the outside length of the pillow edge. Press the raw edges together with wrong sides facing. Refer to New

Options for Gathering Ruffles in the Glossary for methods of gathering. Attach the ruffle to the outside edge.

6. Pin or tape back the ruffle and trim to the front side of the pillow to prevent them from getting sewn into the front/back seam. Cut a backing the same size as the front. With right sides facing each other, pin the layers together, keeping the pillow front wrong side up. Stitch through all the layers, sewing in the seamline used to attach the ruffle. Put a size 14/90 needle in your machine to stitch through all the layers. Clip across the outside points before reversing. Reverse. Remove the tape or pins holding the ruffle.

7. Insert a pillow form into the pillow and hand-stitch the opening closed.

TRAPUNTO ROSE PILLOW PATTERN

Enlarge pattern to 9" across.

26

BOSTON COMMONS TABLECLOTH

The techniques of Seminole strip piecing have numerous applications for home decorating. The tablecovering shown in the photograph is a nice project introducing this method, and I encourage you to use the technique for curtains, valances, or similar applications. This cloth measures $28\frac{1}{2}'' \times 33''$.

MATERIALS

¼ yard of each of three cotton coordinates

1 yard of cotton print for background

1 yard of backing fabric

1 yard of polyester batting

Matching sewing threads

INSTRUCTIONS

1. Cut two $2'' \times 44''$ strips from each of the three cotton coordinates, and three $2'' \times 44''$ strips from the background print. Arrange six strips beginning and ending with a background strip; the inner four will be one of each of the coordinates and one background print. Referring to the color photograph plate 22, the arrangement of color strips viewed from the border to the tablecloth center is: yellow background print/ green/ yellow background print/ purple/ red/ yellow background print. The four inner strips of this band may or may not contain a repeat of the background fabric, according to your own taste. It is important, however, to begin this six-strip construction beginning and ending with the background fabric. This arrangement will create the illusion of the bands floating on the tablecloth center.

2. Sew the strips together using a $\frac{1}{4}''$ seam allowance along their 44'' length into a six-strip band. Press the seams open.

3. Cut the assembled band into 2'' segments cutting across the $9\frac{1}{2}''$ width. Keeping the short end of the ruler even with the outside edge to main-

tain a straight cut, work across the length of the band.

4. The segments will be sewn together using a $\frac{1}{4}''$ seam allowance to construct four borders for the tablecloth. The segments will be arranged as in Seminole piecing, by offsetting the first strip one strip seam down from the preceding segment's outer edge. In my sample I aligned the yellow background strip to the green print. This will result in the sixth and last strip in the segment, the outer yellow background print, extending beyond the edge of the previous segment. Continue to sew the third segment and all following segments, maintaining this position. The resulting band will appear to have a diagonal orientation.

Cut into 2" segments.

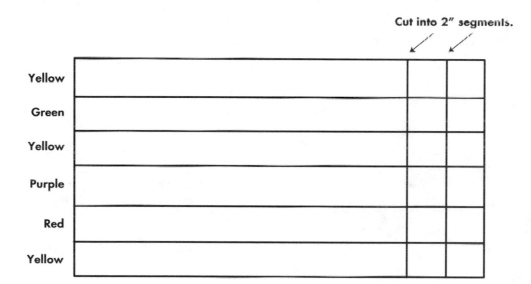

Yellow
Green
Yellow
Purple
Red
Yellow

Reassemble offsetting
one seam.

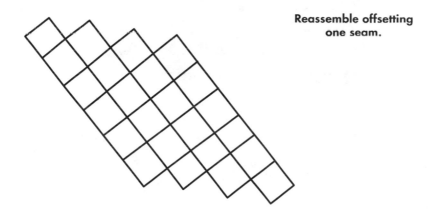

5. The tablecloth photographed is rectangular rather than square. The long side borders required an eight-segment border; the short sides needed six segments. In order to turn the corner of the band, it will be necessary to attach a corner triangle section constructed as shown in the insert diagram below. The insert will connect one border to the next at right angles to each other. Assemble the four border bands together joined with four inserts. Press after stitching.

6. The inside opening of the assembled borders will be completed by appliquéing the entire unit to a background rectangle. Baste the inside triangle edge of the unit to the background triangle, maintaining the points of the top background print of each square. Lay the basted section on a flat surface and carefully measure the inside opening. Overcut the background print for this opening by approximately 1″ overall. Securely pin or baste the rectangle behind the border bands, and appliqué the band to the rectangle using a blindstich and matching thread. Trim away the excess seam allowance after attachment.

7. Cut four 6½″ × 36″ bands from the background print for the outside borders. Sew these bands to the long sides of the tablecloth, trimming the triangle points after stitching. Complete by sewing the outer bands to the two remaining sides of the tablecloth.

8. Cut 2″ strips for the binding. Cut the fabric lengthwise on the grain, parallel to the selvage. Bind the cloth edges, following the instructions in Binding by Machine in the Glossary.

BOSTON COMMONS TABLECLOTH DIAGRAM—BORDER CORNER SEGMENT

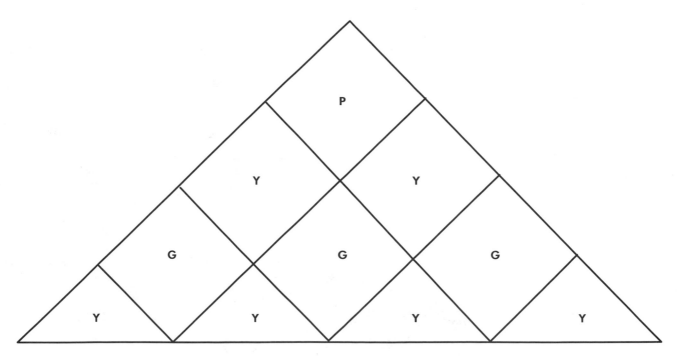

P—print
Y—yellow
G—green

PART FOUR

SHADES

Shades filter light, provide privacy, and are an opportunity for creative design. Lampshades have been featured throughout this book, embellished with appliqués and machine stitchery. The simplest lampshade style for covering is the smooth paper or plastic type available at most craft stores. Inexpensive cardboard or paper lampshades purchased at discount stores are also an option. Practice on a shade you have earmarked for the rubbish, and with a bit of time you will gain the experience and confidence to tackle all styles.

To begin with, you must make a pattern of the outside shell of the shade. Use newspaper taped together to an adequate size or brown wrapping paper. Begin at the shade seam, and mark the outside edges of the cover, slowly turning the shade to trace the entire perimeter of its shape. Complete the tracing at the end of the seam. Cut out the pattern and test it by overlaying the paper on the lampshade to determine if you have accurately drawn the outline. Adjust the shape as needed. There are lampshades available at the larger craft stores that come with a pattern of their shape. Once you have made the pattern you can determine the yardage required to cover the shade. You are now ready to follow the generic directions beginning on the following page.

27
LAMPSHADE

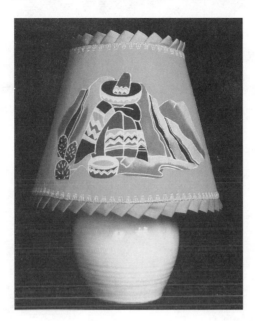

As you will see from these directions, lampshades can take as little as an hour's time to complete. Make a shade for every holiday, storing them flat when not in use.

MATERIALS

Fabric in yardage sufficient to cover the lamp-shade plus a ½" seam allowance on the outer curves and a 1" seam allowance at the joining straight edge

Firm fusible interfacing such as Craft Decor by Pellon™ in the same quantity as the lamp-shade cover fabric

Bound-edge trimming of piping, lace, or ruffling in the total length of the top and bottom outside curves

Hook-and-loop tape the length of one straight side

Matching sewing threads

INSTRUCTIONS

1. Trace the shade pattern onto the heavy-weight interfacing. Cut out the interfacing the same size as the pattern.

2. Following the interfacing manufacturer's directions, fuse the interfacing to the wrong side of the lampshade fabric.

3. Cut the lampshade fabric out, adding a ¼″ seam allowance around the outside (top and bottom) curved edges and a 1″ seam allowance to the straight back seam.

4. Appliqué or embellish the fabric you have chosen for the shade cover at this point. If you are attaching pieced fabric, carry the seams to the two curved edges.

5. Using a bound edging such as piping, position the trim with the raw edges aligned with the outside edge of the shade. Stitch in the seamline

of the trimming. Fold the trim over to the shade's wrong side and topstitch it, holding the seam allowance to the wrong side of the shade. This will provide a finished edge for the lampshade.

6. Sew hook-and-loop tape to the straight edge of the shade to form an overlapped closure.

7. Align the outside with the lampshade foundation and secure the shade in place with the hook-and-loop closure.

28
SOUTHWEST PLEATED WINDOW SHADE

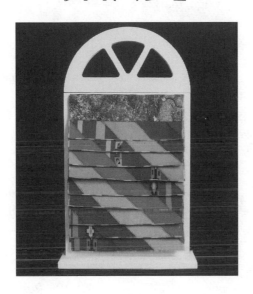

Through the use of color and pattern, this shade has a distinct flavor of the southwestern United States. Decorators have utilized the pleated window shade as a contemporary option for privacy and color accent. You can readily transform the commonplace into this simple yet creative interpretation. The following method of transferring a diagonal design to the surface of a pleated shade is fast and easy to execute. There is no reason to limit the designs for this medium to diagonal lines alone. Any line drawing, be it abstract or representational, could quickly be transferred to the surface of the pleats. Geometrics of any kind are appropriate, but feel free to use pictures of all sorts.

MATERIALS

Naturally the yardage required will vary according to the specific window measurement. In addition to fabrics used on the interior treatment, select a white or light-colored lining layer of cloth. The liner will be seen from the outside and be exposed to fading. The liner will be the measured window width plus 3″ × the measured window length. The interior shade construction will require the window length × 6″ for every pleat.

INSTRUCTIONS

1. For accuracy, tape newspaper together to equal the width of the window opening and at least twice the window length.

2. Three inches down from the top edge, mark a horizontal line across the paper width. Six inches down from that line, mark a second horizontal line across the paper. Check the accuracy of the second line by measuring 6″ down from two points on the first line. Carefully mark a third line across the width of the paper 3″ below the second line. Repeat this procedure until the paper is filled with paired 3″-wide lines that are 6″ apart.

3. Fold the 6″-wide space in half bringing the crease to the third marked line. This folding is similar to making a child's fan. Fold the paper until it is equal to the length of the inside of the window.

4. Once the paper pattern is sufficient in size to the window length and width, you are ready to mark the diagonal motif. Temporarily tape the folds closed to reveal only the 3″ line segments. This is the design surface.

5. Place a quilter's ruler with its 45-degree mark even with the outside short edge of the paper, and mark a line along the long edge of the ruler. Measure 3″ from this drawn diagonal line and mark a series of diagonals parallel to it. Carry the lines across the pleated surface area until they terminate on the opposite outside edge of the paper. Refer to Gridding Lines and Right-Angle Triangles in the Glossary.

6. To determine a color key for the fabrics to be used in the project, use colored pencils on the pleated area. Begin with the left top edge and shade in one color. Moving across the paper, shade the next diagonal area, which runs into the second or third pleated segments, with a sec-

ond color. Use as many colors on the paper as necessary to clarify the various fabrics you will use. To minimize confusion, mark the top pleated segment A, the second B, and so forth for each pleat surface.

7. The design fabric used on the surface of the pleats will be fused to a base fabric. Using Wonder-Under™, position the paper side over the markings, carefully tracing all the colored areas for your first fabric. As you trace the lines of each area, mark the color #1 as well as the row A, B, etc., for positioning the fused fabric.

8. Mark the master pattern with the same number and letter codes to correspond to the Wonder-Under. I found it easiest to trace each row without cutting until all the row lines were marked. Cut the fusible Wonder-Under on the lines and put the pieces into separate envelopes coded for each color group.

9. Untape the paper pattern to open the pleated design surface. Cut the fabric needed for the full length of the interior of the pleated shade.

10. Transfer the horizontal lines to the base fabric. Lay the paper pattern next to the base fabric. Begin 8″ down from the top, and mark clearly the same 3″/6″ spacing sequence.

11. Transfer the Wonder-Under to the appropriate design fabrics. Remove the paper backing and, following the manufacturer's directions, fuse the first color in place in all the rows you have indicated for its placement. Repeat this process for the remaining colors until all the pleated surface areas are filled with the fused colors.

12. Add decorative stitching between the diagonal rows of fabric for additional accent. In the photograph the lower edge of each horizontal pleated row was accented further with a serged rolled hem executed with a variegated Woolly Nylon™ thread.

13. Layer the lining fabric under the base fabric.

14. Finish the long sides of the lining fabric with a rolled serger hem or a hem on your sewing machine.

15. Form the fabric pleats in the same manner as you did the pleated paper pattern. Topstitch the pleat ⅛″ with a straight stitch or make a rolled serger seam at the pleat edge. Continue until all the pleats are sewn. Retain a flat 6″ section of the base fabric below the last pleat.

16. Fold the 6″ of fabric beneath the last pleat to form a casing along the bottom of the shade and insert a wooden dowel or slat into it. The weighted casing will maintain the form of the lower shade edge.

17. Use Dritz™ Iron-on Shade Loop Tape and press it onto the lining fabric edge and the window frame. Follow the manufacturer's directions for properly installing the loop tape.

18. String cording through the loops for drawing the shade in the following manner: Tie a cord at one end and insert the other end through each vertical row of loops, secured at each lower edge loop. Draw the cords horizontally through the loops at the top edge until all meet on one side. Knot the cords together, unifying their length, and draw the cords as one unit to raise and lower the shade. Treat the cord ends with Fray Check™.

29
ROSETTE BALLOON WINDOW SHADE

Balloon shades are a standard window treatment that offer another opportunity for embellishment. With the availablity of iron-on or sew-in ring tape, the shade can be made in an afternoon.

INSTRUCTIONS

Measure the window opening and double the width for adequate fullness. Double the window opening length for the shade length.

To prevent fading it is recommended that you line the shade. Cut the lining the same length as the shade less 2″ in width. Sew the lining and shade together using a ¼″ seam allowance along the long sides and the lower edge. Reverse and press. Since the shade is wider than the lining, a framing border of the shade fabric should wrap over to the wrong side. Bring the lower edge up 1″ and stitch parallel to the lower edge, creating a casing. The casing provides a pocket to insert a

dowel or weighted chain along the lower edge. This gives adequate weight to the shade bottom for the shade to function properly.

Position the iron-on or sew-in Roman shade tape 1¾″ from the finished side edge, overlapping the lower edge by ¼″. Be certain to start the lower edge with a ring. Attach the tape in place, after stitching the lining and shade layers together. Stitch along the tape placement line, allowing the double layer of fabric to draw as one unit. When you are constructing an unlined shade, the fusible ring tape is adequately strong to eliminate sewing. Space and pin the remaining rows of tape across the shade at invervals of 18″ to 36″. The spacing will depend on the size of the window as well as the number of pouf rows you wish to create. Working in vertical rows, thread cord through the tape. Draw each row across to the outside top ring you will be using to operate the shade. Since the cords will vary in length depending on their distance from the single end location, knot all the cords together and trim the ends to a uniform length. Secure all the cord ends with Fray Check™.

Pull the shade up, adjusting the folds and gathers until they are even. For each rosette, cut out the pattern provided, keeping the fold of the pattern on the bias of the fabric. Bring the curved edge together with wrong sides to the inside, and sew a long running stitch along it. Starting at one raw edge, curve the shape around your finger as you draw the basting stitches taut. Once the flower shape is achieved, sew the raw edges together and wrap the threads around the fabric ends to maintain the flower shape. Interface the leaves to achieve a stiff shape. Line each leaf, and reverse. Topstitch the leaf opening to minimize hand sewing. Sew leaf pairs behind each rosette and secure the layers together. With matching thread, sew the flowers inside the pouf sections of the balloon shade in a pleasing arrangement.

ROSETTE BALLOON WINDOW SHADE PATTERN

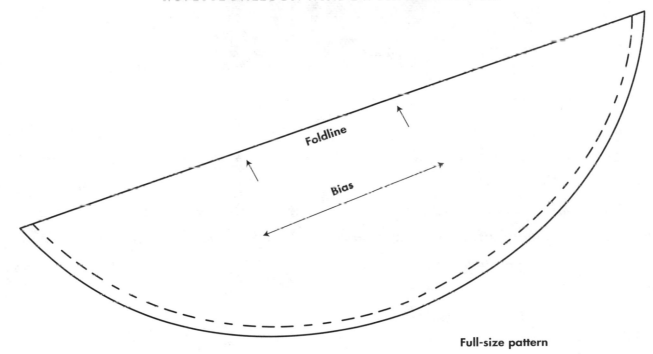

Foldline

Bias

Full-size pattern

30
A BEAR'S FAIRY-TALE WINDOW SHADE

What could be more fun than transforming an evening window into a canvas for your child's imagination? In the picture of the Holiday Place Mats and table setting, plate 25 in the color insert, the holiday cheer is enhanced by a Christmas window shade. The fundamentals of shade construction are the same for this project, but the opportunity for using the medium for an appliqué picture is explored here in greater detail. With the availability of Wonder-Shade™, you can fuse a shade treatment in minutes, and insulate the window from temperature and light at the same time. The outer layer, which is exposed to the outside, remains a white vinyl layer. This is backed to a fusible layer that will be the bonding agent to the wall hanging. If you do not presently have a shade for your window, purchase an inexpensive shade cut to the correct window size for either inside or flush mounting. You will need the roller and its mechanism; you'll remove and discard the shade material.

Construct the shade following the specific directions for this design. Complete all the appliqué and embroidery on the background fabric. Fuse the background fabric to the Wonder-Shade following the manufacturer's directions. Trim the Wonder-Shade to the size of the removed shade. Before permanently securing the shade to the roller

I like to preview its placement by temporarily anchoring the new shade to the dowel with masking tape. Check to see if it is correctly positioned, adjust the shade, and, finally, permanently install the shade with a staple gun.

MATERIALS

Blue background fabric sufficient in length to cover entire shade

7" circle of yellow solid for moon

⅛ yard gold tissue lamé

Heatnbond™ fusible transfer product

Small quantity of beige and rust print for quilt appliqué and solids for balloon appliqués

Matching sewing and embroidery threads

Freezer paper

INSTRUCTIONS

1. Enlarge the patterns for the appliqués to the size indicated on page 98 with the use of a copy machine.

2. Lay the yellow moon fabric over the pattern and use colored indelible marking pens to transfer the facial features to the fabric and to mark the circle before trimming the appliqué to its finished size. It will be easy to appliqué the moon using the Layered Machine Appliqué method explained in the Glossary.

3. Trace the enlarged patterns for the hot air balloon and the boat to freezer paper as detailed in the appliqué instructions in the Glossary. Iron the freezer paper to the wrong side of the background fabric once you have determined the location that will work best for your window shade. Appliqué using the method detailed in the Glossary.

4. Heatnbond is a fusible transfer product that does not require stitching. Following the manufacturer's directions, the product can be successfully fused without fear of the appliqué's coming away from the background. The appliqué will be stiff in texture, but that is fine for this project. Using tissue lamé, fuse the Heatnbond to the wrong side of the lamé. Trace an assortment of stars to the paper side of the Heatnbond. Cut the stars out and remove the paper backing from the appliqués. Protecting the stars with a pressing cloth, position and press the stars to the background.

5. Before removing the freezer paper layer from the wrong side of the background, complete all the embroidery and appliqué stitching. Heavy threads may be wound in the bobbin of the sewing machine and stitched with the needle to the wrong side of the drawing. Heavy threads worked with a simple straight stitch will embellish the right side of the shade. This method was used to creat the roping of the balloon as well as the waves alongside the boat. Facial details on the bears were added with a fine-line indelible marking pen.

6. When all the stitching is completed, remove the freezer paper and any additional stabilizer that may be on the wrong side of the shade. This material will affect the bond of the shade.

7. Following the manufacturer's directions, for the Wonder-Shade, press the appliqué picture to the shade fabric. Use a protective layer on the ironing board, and a thin pressing cloth on the wall hanging side. Use steam, and press the layers for at least seven seconds in each location. Check for spots that have not sufficiently bonded and apply additional steam. Air bubbles can be released by a small pinprick to the white side of the shade material.

8. Allow the shade to cool several minutes.

9. Using a rotary cutter, carefully measure and trim the shade.

10. Using masking tape, secure the new shade to the roller. Check to see if it is properly positioned. When you are pleased with the application, complete the installation by tacking the shade to the roller with a staple gun.

11. Turn under 1″ on the lower end of the shade. Stitch this casing by machine with matching thread. When the shade is hung, install a wooden dowel in the casing. Restrict stitching on the shade front to this one row of machine stitching, as each additional stitch will create a puncture in the shade material.

A BEAR'S FAIRY-TALE WINDOW SHADE PATTERNS

Enlarge to 13″ length.

Enlarge to 13″ height.

SEQUENCE 1. BINDING BY MACHINE

1. Cut the binding parallel with the selvage lengthwise on the fabric grain when binding a straight-sided edge. While binding width may vary, this method is easiest to accomplish with a binding cut 2¼″ wide. To piece strips together for a required length, position the ends, with right sides facing each other, at right angles to each other as shown in the photograph.

2. On the wrong side of the top strip, draw a stitching line that begins at the top right corner diagonally across the corner area to the lower left edge of the top fabric.

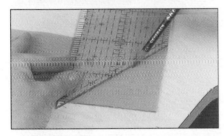

3. On the marked line sew with a short stitch length, 2 mm or 15 stitches per inch.

4. Open the strip to a continuous band and trim the excess seam allowance ¼″ away from the seamline.

5. Using steam, iron the band in half, with the wrong sides of the fabric facing each other.

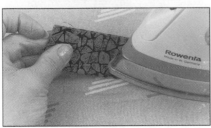

6. Trim the edges of the quilt even. Align the raw edges of the binding to the quilt's raw edge. Start in the middle of one side, leaving an unattached tail of binding of at least 3″ long for attaching the binding into one band.

7. When approaching the corner, stop ½″ from the next side edge, and keep the needle in a down position. Rotate the work 90 degrees. Sew in reverse to have the needle behind the seam, and the fabric clear for manipulation.

8. Fold the binding over into a triangular shape with the fold even with the preceding side, and the raw edge of the binding even with the new side.

9. Reenter the seamline with the needle, maintaining a ¼″ seam allowance from the outside edge. Sew all the corners in the same manner. Join the two binding ends together by overlaying the ends to mark seam placement. Open the binding layers flat, and sew the two ends together. Complete seaming the ends to the quilt layers.

10. When the binding fold is brought to the wrong side, a mitered corner will show on the right side.

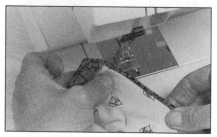

11. On the wrong side, bring the binding fold ¼″ beyond the seamline.

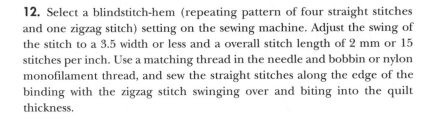

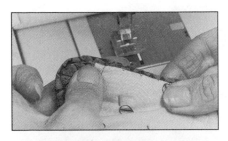

12. Select a blindstitch-hem (repeating pattern of four straight stitches and one zigzag stitch) setting on the sewing machine. Adjust the swing of the stitch to a 3.5 width or less and a overall stitch length of 2 mm or 15 stitches per inch. Use a matching thread in the needle and bobbin or nylon monofilament thread, and sew the straight stitches along the edge of the binding with the zigzag stitch swinging over and biting into the quilt thickness.

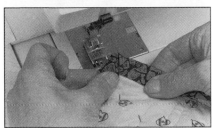

13. After blindstitching along one side, fold the corners under, forming a miter on the wrong side. This can be reinforced later with a narrow zigzag stitch worked in matching thread or nylon monofilament thread.

14. The blindstitch will be invisible from the quilt front. Another option for stitching the binding by machine is to fold over ¼″ beyond the seamline on the wrong side and to topstitch in the ditch on the right side of the quilt with invisible thread or a matching color.

SEQUENCE 2. MAKING PIPING

1. Measure a length along the selvage end and fold the fabric diagonally over as shown until the lower end of the triangle formed is the same length as the left short side of the triangle. Pin the corners in place to prevent movement.

2. Cut in the diagonal fold. The edge created from the fold is true bias.

3. Cut strips on the bias of the cloth. In most cases, strips cut 1¼″ in width will be a workable size for seam insertion. Bias binding strips are commonly cut 1½″ in width, but this width will require trimming when used for piping. Check a sample before cutting and constructing the amount required for your project.

4. Install the zipper foot on the sewing machine and adjust the needle position accordingly.

5. Position the cording in the center of the wrong side of the cut bias.

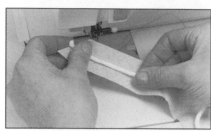

6. Stitch with the needle as close as possible to the cording to create the piping.

SEQUENCE 3. SPIRAL PATCHWORK

1. Assemble strips cut lengthwise along the grain, parallel to the selvage of the fabric, into a unit. The strips should be as long as possible without seaming, and sewn using a $\frac{1}{4}''$ seam allowance. Press the fabric created flat, with the seams to one side.

2. Fold the short side over diagonally as shown in the photograph until its top edge is even with the opposite outside raw edge.

3. Insert the sewing machine needle $\frac{1}{4}''$ from the raw edges of the lower right corner of the folded triangle as shown.

4. Keeping the needle in the down position, raise the presser foot of the machine and bring the left side's raw edge even to the right side's long raw edge. You will be able to align only a short distance of several inches.

5. Sew using a ¼″ seam allowance, twisting the sides to maintain their alignment.

6. When the seam is completed you will have a tube as shown in the photo, made of the varied strips of cloth.

7. Press the tube flat, and cut it open along one of the creases.

8. The resulting yardage will have double the width of the previous bands, and the strips will appear as through they had been tediously constructed on the bias one at a time. This yardage is ideal for tiebacks or borders, or to cut into rainbow bias.

9. The tieback shown was cut from a spiral section.

SEQUENCE 4. GRIDDING LINES AND RIGHT-ANGLE TRIANGLES

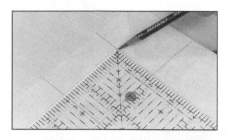

1. On the wrong side of one layer of fabric that will be used in the pieced triangle construction, mark a horizontal and vertical grid. If the completed right-angle triangle should finish to 2″, the grid lines will be 2⅞″ apart including seam allowance. For a 3″ finished triangle, grid 3⅞″, adding ⅞″ to the finished size for half-square or right-angle triangle construction.

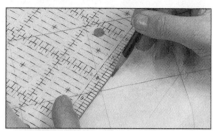

2. Mark lines intersecting the diagonal of the squares.

3. Position the marked fabric with its right side to the right side of its companion fabric. Pin the layers securely. Stitch through both layers, ¼″ on either side of the marked diagonal lines.

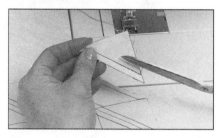

4. When sewing is completed, cut the triangles apart on the marked lines.

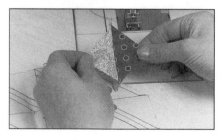

5. Open the sewn section to reveal the constructed square.

SEQUENCE 5. MARKING A GRIDDED QUILTING PATTERN

1. Use a chalk marker or soft lead pencil when gridding quilting lines. Draw the lines parallel to the edge of the quilt using a quilters' ruler.

2. Lay the short edge of the ruler on a previously drawn line to establish lines intersecting at right angles. Intersect the triangles for a diagonal line. Remember to keep at least one side of the ruler on a previously drawn line to make all lines parallel to previous markings.

SEQUENCE 6. HEMMING A CURTAIN

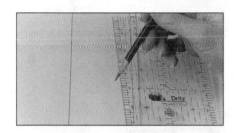

1. On cardboard or paper, carefully mark a line ¼″ in from the edge and parallel to it, and another line 3″ from the edge (parallel to it and to the first drawn line) as shown.

2. Trim the edges clean and press the raw edge of the curtain over the marked paper, bringing ¼″ over to the first marked line.

3. Reposition the curtain edge, bringing the creased fold to the 3″ marked line on the paper or cardboard. Press. This will prepare the hem edge for stitching.

4. Pin the folded hem at regular intervals and sew the lower edge of the curtain to complete the construction.

SEQUENCE 7. INSTALLING PLEATER OR SHIRRING TAPE

1. Press a ½″ seam allowance over to the wrong side of the curtain edge.

2. For Dritz™ Iron–on Pleater Tape, use a steam iron to press the tape in place ¼″ below the top edge. Free the cords before trimming the tape and knot the ends together.

3. For Gosling™ or Montserrat™ tape, which is sewn into place, place the tape ¼″ from curtain's top edge.

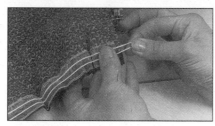

4. Sew using a matching thread in the indicated seam guides on the tape. Sew tape ends along both the lower and the top edges of the tape. Draw both cords at once to pleat the tape. Secure the ends and treat the cord ends with Fray Check™.

SEQUENCE 8. LAYERED MACHINE APPLIQUÉ

1. Use freezer paper, available at most grocery stores, to transfer the appliqué pattern. Position the coated side of the paper up, with the appliqué drawing under the paper. Use an indelible fine-line marking pen to transfer all the pattern lines to the coated side of the paper.

2. Prepare the appliqué fabric by spray-starching on both sides until the fabric is stiff. Make certain that the appliqué fabric is at least 2″ larger overall than the finished appliqué size. Starch all fabrics, no matter how small, before using for this method.

3. Fill the bobbin of your sewing machine with ThreadFuse™.

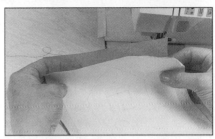

4. Iron the coated side of the freezer paper to the wrong side of the background fabric. Position the appliqué fabric right side out on the front side of the background fabric. Be certain to cover the line drawing of the design, as indicated by the freezer paper guide.

5. On the wrong side of the cloth, sew with a straight stitch on the line drawing of the first appliqué. Stitch length should be 3 mm or 10 stitches per inch. The appliqué illustrated is the small Delph house featured on the curtains in color plate 6. The first fabric to be stitched down is the large house shape. The windows and doors will be applied after, over this section. For this step, use a neutral-colored thread for the needle, with the ThreadFuse in the bobbin.

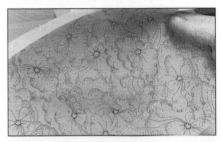

6. Cut the threads after sewing. The ThreadFuse will be clearly visible on the right side of your work.

7. Remove the bobbin filled with ThreadFuse and replace it with a thread that matches the color in the needle.

8. Set the machine for a satin stitch. The stitch length should be very close, with a narrow zigzag of 2 mm or less. Lighten the needle tension to approximately two adjustments less than the setting for a balanced straight stitch. If your sewing machine has the option of a needle-down position, this is an excellent time to utilize this feature. Use a thread color that matches the appliqué fabric as closely as possible. Satin-stitch over the ThreadFuse. The stitch should be dense enough to completely encase the ThreadFuse.

9. Use small embroidery scissors or appliqué scissors as shown to trim away the excess fabric. If you are right-handed, work in a clockwise movement with the lower blade against the satin stitching. Left-handed operators must work counterclockwise. Barely open the blades of the scissors; use only the sharp tip to minimize the risk of cutting into the background fabric. Hold your hand with the palm facing up and gently glide the scissor tip to trim away the excess fabric. Your thumb and ring finger should be in the finger holders of the scissors. With your other hand you can be holding the fabric taut. This motion will eliminate most, if not all, of the appliqué fabric threads from the satin-stitched area.

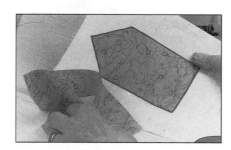

10. After the appliqué is complete, press the work with a steam iron following the ThreadFuse manufacturer's directions. This fusible agent will melt within the satin stitching and reinforce the fabric/thread bond. This will make the appliqué sufficiently strong for you to trim away the layers of appliqué and background fabric stitched beneath the top surface. In the case of the Delph House curtains, doing this will eliminate the shadowing of layers as sunlight comes through the window. For quilted projects, this method will allow for hand or machine quilting or the addition of embroidery details to the appliqué. The completed project is softer and more pleasing to the touch.

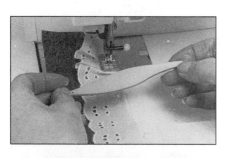

11. Add additional layers of appliqué and surface stitching as the freezer paper guide suggests. The paper will serve as your pattern and embroidery guide as well as an inexpensive stabilizer through the project. When all the stitchery is completed, remove the paper. Trim away the layers, and remove any additional fuzzy threads from the satin stitching on the right side.

SEQUENCE 9. NEW OPTIONS FOR GATHERING RUFFLES

1. A handy new tool for keeping fingers out of harm's way when stitching, as well as when pleating and gathering fabrics, is the Puts-It™. It is curved, has a convenient ruler on one end, a needle inserter eye, and is grooved for added control in grabbing fabric.

2. Without too much preparation align the prepared ruffle and lay the flat end of the Puts-It under the presser foot of the sewing machine. If you maintain a consistent pleat depth, this little device will help to make a professional and generous ruffle in no time at all. With it, attaching a flat eyelet trim to the raw edge of ruffling fabric, as shown, becomes a one-step operation.

3. For the conventional sewing machine, the traditional ruffler attachment is always a fast and excellent approach to creating a ruffle. The attachment has a series of numbers and a star on a movable gauge on the ruffle front. The numbers are one through twelve. One refers to the attachment's making a ruffle or pleat for every stitch. The gauge can be set at the number six, denoting a ruffle for every six stitches, and, finally, at twelve for a more open ruffle with a pleat every twelve stitches. The star groove allows an interruption in pleating. This is convenient for attaching additional yardage to a ruffle without the time-consuming operation of removing the attachment. The most common setting is six. Be aware that since these settings are synchronized to the stitch-per-inch setting, the pleating will be directly altered by the movement of the feed dogs of the sewing machine. Lengthening and shortening the stitch settings on the sewing machine will modify the ruffle as well. Practice on sample cloth until you are familiar with changes in settings on the ruffle gauge and the machine's stitch length. Whatever fabric is placed between the ruffler blades will gather. Whatever fabric is placed under the attachment will not gather. You can gather the ruffle and attach it with one step. This requires some dexterity, but a few hours are sufficient to master this most convenient technique.

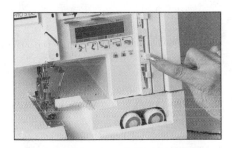

4. Sergers equipped with differential feed adjustments provide an additional method for gathering. Refer to your serger manual and increase the feed to a plus setting of 2 as shown in our photograph. This will allow for a ratio of two-to-one, doubling the ruffle fullness.

5. Feed the fabric with a 3- or 4-thread overlocking stitch and it will be ruffled.

6. Increasing the needle tension may provide you with additional fullness. Experiment with fabric weight and settings to achieve the fullness you seek.

7. Some sergers feature accessory feet that allow for gathering the layer closest to the feed dog while attaching with an overlock stitch a second layer that remains unshirred. This provides a fast one-step application.

SEQUENCE 10. USING A FASTURN™

1. Cut strips of fabric, either on the bias or straight along the grain lengthwise or crosswise. Sew the raw edges together with the right sides of the fabric facing each other. Use a ¼″ to ⅛″ seam allowance for seaming. The Fasturn™ foot holds the raw edges together securely as the strip is sewn, minimizing error.

2. Select a Fasturn tube size that allows the fabric tube to easily slide down on the outside of the it. If the strips are cut on the bias, the tube will allow for up to a 2-yard length to be reversed easily.

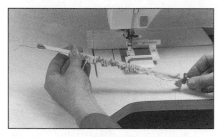

3. Insert the matching-size looped wire through the center of the tube and turn the loop in a clockwise motion, catching the raw fabric edge.

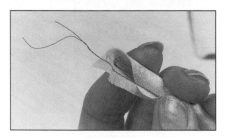

4. Pull the fabric into the tube using the wire.

5. The fabric will quickly slide through the tube and reverse itself out the opposite end. You may insert batting or cording into the tube at the same time as you reverse the fabric.

6. For the appliqué treatments most commonly used in this book, press the seam to the center of the back side of the trim.

SEQUENCE 11. MACHINE TRAPUNTO

1. Use the two-ply nylon yarn commonly sold for gift wrapping.

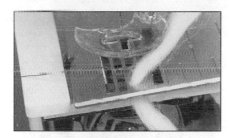

2. Cut a convenient length of approximately 12″. Separate the yarn into one ply.

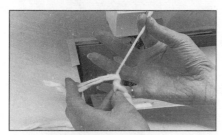

3. Bring the cording up through the small hole in the throat plate of your sewing machine. You may use a looper threader to help feed this cord through the threading path of the throat plate.

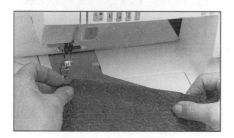

4. Prepare the sewing machine by inserting a double needle. The Trapunto Rose Pillow used in this book was worked with a 4.0 mm double needle. This size allowed for the successful feeding of the cord weight indicated. Straight-line cording can be accomplished with a pintucking foot on the machine and the feed dog in a raised position. The curved lines of the design provided in the trapunto project were accomplished with the feed dog lowered; a hoop and a darning foot were used on the machine. The foot shown in the photograph is the Bigfoot™. This is an excellent accessory that allows for maximum visibility and control and is available for most sewing machine models.

5. The trapunto work should be accomplished before the layers of the projects are assembled for quilting. When removing the fabric from the machine, cut the cording as well as the threads.

SEQUENCE 12. FRENCH SEAMS

1. Position the fabric with the wrong sides facing each other and raw edges aligned.

2. Sew the layers wrong sides together using a ⅛″ seam allowance. Press the seam to one side.

3. Refold the fabric with the right sides of the fabric facing each other, carefully enclosing the seam centered in the foldline.

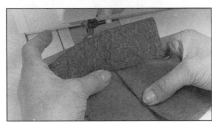

4. Stitch with right sides facing each other using a ¼″ seam allowance. Continue to sew this seam flat with further construction.

SEQUENCE 13. LINING A CURTAIN AND PREPARING THE HEADER

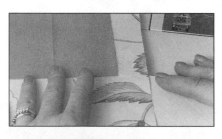

1. Cut the lining 2″ less in width and length than the finished curtain. The curtain fabric will wrap around to the lining side after sewing, preventing the lining from showing along the side edges of the curtain.

2. Position the lining and curtain with right fabric sides facing and side edges even. The lining will be positioned at the finished longwise edge of the curtain fabric with the hem extending beyond. Sew the sides together with a 1 ½″ seam allowance.

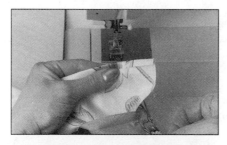

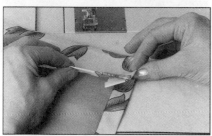

3. Reverse and press the sides flat. Press ¼″ over along the lower raw edge of the hem.

4. Fold the hem to its finished size with top hem edges held against each other and side edges even and flat.

5. Sew the hem ⅛″ from the edge with matching threads. Use nylon monofilament thread in the bobbin for a multicolored fabric.

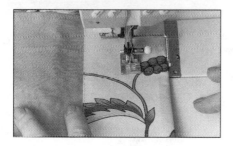

6. To eliminate marking the rod casing along the curtain header, use the quilting guide on your sewing machine. Measure the distance from the top edge to the top rod pocket stitching line. Adjust the quilting guide distance from the needle to this width, and tighten the guide into position.

7. Align the top edge of the curtain with guide bar of the attachment and sew, maintaining this distance.

SEQUENCE 14. PIECING ON A SERGER (ROLLED HEM)

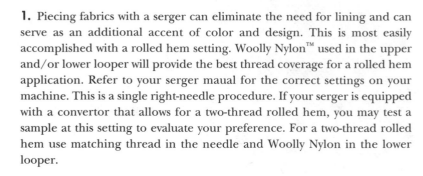

1. Piecing fabrics with a serger can eliminate the need for lining and can serve as an additional accent of color and design. This is most easily accomplished with a rolled hem setting. Woolly Nylon™ used in the upper and/or lower looper will provide the best thread coverage for a rolled hem application. Refer to your serger maual for the correct settings on your machine. This is a single right-needle procedure. If your serger is equipped with a convertor that allows for a two-thread rolled hem, you may test a sample at this setting to evaluate your preference. For a two-thread rolled hem use matching thread in the needle and Woolly Nylon in the lower looper.

2. Position the fabric with wrong sides facing each other and raw edges even.

3. Serge along the edge, trimming away a scant seam allowance.

4. On the right sides of the fabric the rolled hem is clearly visible.

5. The wrong side is cleanly finished. The sides are reversible as you see fit, and they will withstand frequent laundering.

SEQUENCE 15. ATTACHING BEADS WITH A SERGER

1. Accessory feet are available for most model sergers for the attachment of beads and piping. The foot for this application provides a channel for the beads to rest in during the overlocking procedure. This is most commonly executed with a three-thread overlock stitch, using the right needle for narrow beads, the left needle for wider ones. If the manufacturer of your serger does not offer this product you can purchase a generic foot, which is available to fit many models. In addition to beading and piping, use this foot to apply heavy corded trims. You may use nylon monofilament thread in either or both loopers for the least visibility.

2. The tissue box cover in the Appliqué Shower Curtain Set, page 68, was made using this application.